개정증보

펼치면 항공영어가 보인다

Airline Service English

차 석 빈 지음

백산출판사

Preface

하늘을 나는 것은 인간 모두의 꿈이다. 버스, 철도 등의 교통시설과 국가 간의 이동을 수월하게 하기 위해 등장한 비행기는 이러한 인간의 심리를 자극했고, 그리하여 오랜 시간이 소요되는 육상 및 해상운송보다는 빠르고 안전한 항공운송이 고객을 항공세계로 이끌었으며, 또한 항공업의 발전을 가져왔다.

이러한 항공업의 발전과 궤를 같이하여 많은 사람들이 성 어거스틴(St. Augustine)의 "세상은 한 권의 책이다. 집에서 머물려는 사람은 단지 한 페이지밖에 읽지 못한다"는 구절처럼 보다 넓은 세계를 동경하여 항공업에 종사하고 있으며, 또한 종사하기를 원하고 있다.

본서는 이러한 욕구를 인식하여 다음과 같은 두 가지 의도로 집필되었다. 첫째는 필자가 지금까지의 항공영어를 강의하면서 아쉬워했던 내용의 체계화와 미흡한 부분에 대한 보완작업의 필요성을 느껴서였고, 둘째는 이 분야를 전공하는 학생들은 물론 일선 항공사의 종사자 및 이 분야에 관심이 있는 일반 독자들에게 항공영어 전반에 대한 핵심적인 내용들을 항공영어 흐름도에 맞춰 소개하고자 준비되었다.

본서의 체계는 모두 다섯 부분으로 구성되었다.

Part I은 Check-In 부분으로 항공승무원이 손님의 항공예약을 받는 시점에서부터 손님이 탑승하기 전까지 나누게 되는 대화내용과 공항 내에서 이루어지는 안내방송을 다루었다. Part II는 Before Take-Off 부분으로 승무원이 손님의 비행기 탑승에서부터 비행기 이륙까지 나누게 되는 대화내용과 그 과정에서의 기내 안내방송을 다루었다. Part III는 본서의 가장 핵심부분이라 할 수 있는 비행도중에 승무원과 손님들 사이의 기내 서비스와 관련된 대화내용들과 기내 안내방송을 다루었다. Part IV는 Check-Out 부분으로 손님이 CIQ(세관, 입국 및 검역)를 받고 공항에서 출국하는 과정에서의 대화내용과 공항 내에서 이루어지는 안내방송을 다루었다. 마지막으로, Part V에서는 Part I에서부터 Part VI까지에서 나타나는 항공관련 용어들과 승무원들의 손님응대에 관한 내용을 수록하였다.

저자는 영어를 전공하면서 여행항공영어를 강의한 경험과 해외여행 경험을 살려 이 책을 집필하는 과정에서 항공분야에 관심을 가진 독자들과 관련업계에 도움이 되는 알찬 내용이 되게끔 나름대로 산고(産苦)의 고통과 노력을 기울였으나 막상 열어놓고 보니 부끄러울 따름이다. 부족한 부분은 여러 선배, 동학제현(同學諸賢)의 충고와 지도편달을 바탕으로 보완·발전시켜 나아갈 것을 약속드린다.

끝으로, 이 책이 출간되기까지 가까이에서 격려해 주신 동료교수님들, 표지도안에 도움을 준 THIS(관광정보연구원)의 정지현 실장, 그리고 관광분야에 각별한 관심과 애정을 가지고 본서의 출판을 흔쾌히 승낙해주신 백산출판사 진욱상 사장님과 편집부 직원 여러분에게도 진심으로 감사드린다.

2007. 8.

차석빈

Contents

PART 1 CHECK-IN

PART 4 CHECK-OUT

항공영어 흐름도

	Airline Service English		Airport / In-flight Announcements
PART 01 **CHECK-IN** **(탑승 수속)**	**CHAPTER 1 Check-in Service English** ● Reservation(예약) ● Ticketing(티켓팅) ● Check-In(탑승 수속) ● Security Check-In(보안 수속) ● Reguest of connecting flight(연결편 문의) ● Reguest of boarding station(탑승구 문의) ● Pre-boarding station(탑승구 입구)	↔	**CHAPTER 2 Check-in Announcements** ● Announcement in the airport(공항 내 안내방송) ● Government formalities for departure(출국 수속) ● Check-in(탑승 수속: 국제선 2시간 전, 국내선 1시간 전) ● Security check-in(보안 수속: 출발 20~30분 전) ● Final call for security check-in (보안 수속 마지막 호출: 출발 10분 전) ● Departure delayed(출발편 지연) ● Departure cancelled(출발편 결항) ● Boarding(탑승)
PART 2 **BEFORE TAKE-OFF** **(이륙 준비)**	**CHAPTER 3 Before Take-off Service English** ● Passenger boarding(손님 탑승) ● Seating arrangements(좌석 배정) ● Carry-on baggage(기내 휴대품) ● Smoking and No Smoking(흡연과 금연) ● Preparation for take-off(이륙 준비)	↔	**CHAPTER 4 Before take-off Announcements** ● Boarding(탑승: 80% 완료 시점) ● Take-off delayed(이륙 지연) ● Welcome(환영인사) ● Safety demonstration(비상사태 안전시범) ● Take-off(이륙) ● Restriction on using electronic devices (전자기기 사용제한)
PART 3 **EN-ROUTE** **(기내서비스)**	**CHAPTER 5 En-route Service English** ● Earphone and Towel service(이어폰과 물수건 서비스) ● Meal and beverage service(식음료 서비스) ● In-flight entertainment(기내 오락서비스) ● Service and comfort(서비스와 편의제공) ● Sick passenger handling(환자 서비스) ● In-flight sales(기내 면세품 판매) ● CIQ Information(세관, 입국 및 검역 안내) ● Destination city information(목적지 안내) ● Landing and deplane(착륙과 손님의 비행기 내림)	↔	**CHAPTER 6 En-route Announcements** ● Service plan(전체 서비스 안내) ● Seatbelt sign off(좌석벨트 착용 표시등 꺼짐) ● Meal and leverage(식음료 서비스) ● In-flight movie(기내 영화 상영) ● Turbulence(기체 흔들림) ● In-flight duty-free sales(기내 면세품 판매) ● Doctor/Nurse(응급환자 발생 및 기내 의사 호출) ● Wake-up&Meal service(식사 제공) ● Flying over scenic spots(관광명소 통과) ● Document(입국서류 작성) ● Earphone collection(이어폰 회수: Approach sign 전) ● Destination approaching(목적지 접근: Approach sign 후) ● Landing(착륙) ● Farewell(작별) ● Deplaning(손님의 비행기 내림)
PART 04 **CHECK-OUT** **(입국안내)**	**CHAPTER 7 Check-out Service English** ● Immigration(입국절차) ● Baggage claim(짐 찾기) ● Baggage problems(짐과 관련된 문제) ● Customs(세관 통과) ● Porter service(포터 서비스) ● Renting a car(렌터카) ● Money exchange counter(환전소)	↔	**CHAPTER 8 Check-out Announcements** ● Arrival(도착) ● Paging(호출) ● Arrival delayed(도착편 지연) ● Arrival cancelled(도착편 결항) ● Divert(임시 착륙) ● Lost & Found(유실물 안내)
PART 5 **TERMINOLOGY/ PASSENGER SERVICE** **(항공영어 모음/ 손님응대)**	**CHAPTER 9 Terminology** ● 항공영어 모음		**CHAPTER 10 Passenger Service** ● 손님의 욕구 ● 일반적인 손님 응대 요령 ● 손님 유형별 응대법

PART 01

CHECK-IN

Chapter 1 Check-in Service English
Chapter 2 Check-in Announcements

Chapter 01

Check-in Service English

탑승예약 ~ 손님 탑승 전 과정의 서비스영어

손님으로부터 예약을 받을 때 예약직원은 날짜와 시간, 좌석(일등석, 이등석 등) 등급, 연락주소, 귀항편 등을 물어보고, 예약접수 끝에는 항상 손님이 요구한 사항들을 반복하여 확인시켜 주어야 한다. 또한 손님이 예약을 변경하거나 취소할 때에도 손님이 요구한 사항들을 반복, 확인시켜 줄 필요가 있다.

고객의 예약과 관련된 문의가 끝나면 'Thank you for calling ______ Airlines. Have a nice day!'라는 표현을 써서 손님에게 감사의 말을 전해 자사에 대한 좋은 이미지를 남긴다.

1. Reservation(예약)

기본 어휘

available	book(ing)	cancel	check-in
confirm	contact	address	fare
flight number	one way(single)	trip	reconfirm
reserve	reservation	return	round trip
schedule	seat	stopover	ticket

1) Receiving reservations(예약 접수)

Dialogue 1 예약 1

A: Airline agent, P: Passenger

A : United Airlines. Jennifer, speaking. May I help you?

P : Yes. I'd like to make a reservation to Los Angeles on July 7, Saturday.

A : O.K. Saturday, July 7, 10 a.m.
We have some seats available.

P : All right. I will take it.

A : O.K. Would you like to book your return flight, too?

P : Yes. I'd like to return on August 5.

A : August 5. Let me see.
Yes, we have some seats available at 2 p.m. What class would you like—economy, business or first?

P : Business class.

A : Any stopovers?

P : No, thank you. What's the fare?

A : The business fare is $ 1,500 round-trip.

P : O.K. I'll take it.

A : Your name and phone number, please?

P : Jeong-sik Kim, (010) 543-4343.

A : How do you spell your first name?

P : J-E-O-N-S-I-K. (or J as in Jack, E as in Elizabeth, O as in Oscar, N as in Nancy, G as in George, S as in Sam, I as in India and K as in Kilo)

A : Yes, sir. Your reservation is made for Flight 053 leaving for Los Angeles on July 7, Saturday at 10 a.m. Your reservation number is ZA105.
Your return reservation on August 5, 2 p.m. is also confirmed. You'll have to reconfirm your reservation at least three days before your departure.
Thank you for calling United Airlines.

P : Thank you. Bye.

Dialogue 2

예약 2

A: Airline agent, P: Passenger

A : Best Travel. Miss Park, speaking. May I help you?

P : I'd like to book a flight to Chicago.

A : When do you want to fly, sir?

P : As soon as possible. Any flights on Saturday?

A : We have two flights at 10 a.m. and 4 p.m.
What time would you prefer?

P : I'll take the 4 p.m. flight.

A : O.K. Do you wish to make a return reservation, too?

P : No. Leave it open, please.

A : What class would you like—coach, business or first?

P : Coach, please.

A : Your name and phone number, please?

P : Sam Cook, (540) 751-3320.

A : Thank you. Your reservation is confirmed for Northwest Flight 202 departing for Chicago Saturday at 4 p.m. Your reservation number is ZA 203.
Please plan to arrive at the airport at least two hours prior to the departure time.

P : I will. Thank you. Bye.

A : Thank you for calling Best Travel. And have a nice day!

Dialogue 3

예약 3

A: Airline agent, P: Passenger

A : Northwest Airlines. May I help you?

P : I'd like to make a reservation for a flight to New York.

A : When would you like to leave?

P : This coming Saturday.
Any flights on Saturday afternoon?

A : Yes, we have one at 5 p.m.

P : I will take it.

A : All right. May I have your name?

P : Steve Kim.

A : O.K. Your reservation is made for Flight 209 leaving for New York Saturday at 8 p.m.
Can you give me your telephone number?

P : Sure. My number is 876-0912.

A : Please be sure to check-in at the airport one hour before your flight is scheduled to leave.

P : Thank you very much.

A : Thank you for calling Northwest Airlines. Have a good day!

2) Changing flight schedules(예약 변경)

Dialogue

A: Airline agent, P: Passenger

A : United Airlines. May I help you?

P : Yes. I'd like to change flights. I'm booked for Flight 402 going to Atlanta tomorrow morning, but I'd like to take an afternoon flight.

A : All right, sir. Let me check if there are any afternoon flights. Just a moment.

P : All right.

(······)

A : We have two flights tomorrow afternoon.

The 1:30 flight is sold out, but we have a few open seats on the 4 p.m. flight.

P : Great. Book me for the 4 p.m. flight, please.

A : O.K. sir, your flight has been changed from 402 to 406 leaving Dallas International Airport at 4 p.m. and arriving in Atlanta at 7:30 p.m.

P : Thank you so much.

A : You're quite welcome, sir.

Thank you for flying United Airlines.

3) Cancelling reservations(예약 취소)

Dialogue

A: Airline agent, P: Passenger

A : Best Travel, Miss Park, speaking. May I help you?

P : I want to cancel my reservation for the flight from Seoul to Chicago on Saturday.

A : Your name, please?

P : Sam Cook.

A : All right. Your reservation is cancelled.

Anything else I can do for you today, sir?

P : No, thanks.

A : You're welcome.

4) Confirming reservations(예약 확인)

Dialogue 1 예약확인

A: Airline agent, P: Passenger

A : United Airlines. May I help you?

P : I'd like to confirm my reservation.

A : Your name and flight number, please?

P : My name is James Kim and my flight number is 209.

A : You are leaving for Atlanta on Friday at 6 p.m., right?

P : Yes.

A : Just a moment, please. O.K. Your reservation is confirmed.

Dialogue 2 예약 재확인 1

A: Airline agent, P: Passenger

A : Northwest Airlines, Jennifer, speaking. May I help you?

P : Yes. I want to reconfirm my booking on the flight to Chicago this Saturday.

A : Yes, sir. Your name, please?

P : I'm Sam Cook.

A : Your reservation is confirmed in coach class. Northwest Airlines Flight 202 on October 7.
Your departure time is 4 p.m. Is that right?

P : All right.

A : May I have your contact address?

P : I'll be staying at the Hilton Hotel.

A : Thank you. Is there anything else I can do for you today, sir?

P : No, that's all. Thank you.

A : OK. Thank you for calling Northwest Airlines.

Dialogue 3 예약 재확인 2

A: Airline agent, P: Passenger

P : I'd like to reconfirm my flight.

A : Date and flight number, please.

P : May 15, Flight 055.

A : Your name, please.

P : James Lee.

A : You're booked on our Flight 055 to Chicago on May 15.

2. Ticketing(티켓팅)

Dialogue 1 예약을 한 경우

A: Airline agent, P: Passenger

A : May I help you?

P : I want to purchase my ticket. I already have a reservation. My reservation number is ZA 205.

A : Your name, please?

P : James Kim.

A : Yes, sir. 4 p.m. Saturday, Northwest Airlines, right?

P : Right. How much is the fare?

A : It's $ 880 for round-trip.

P : Do you accept Visa card?

A : Sure. May I have your credit card, please?

P : Here you are.

(......)

A : Would you like to sign here, please?

P : O.K.

A : Here is your ticket for Seoul, economy class, on Flight 005 leaving at 4 p.m. on July 2nd.

Anything else I can do for you?

P : No. Thanks, anyway.

A : You're welcome. Have a nice day!

Dialogue 2

예약을 하지 않은 경우

A: Airline agent, P: Passenger

A : Good morning. May I help you, sir?

P : I want to purchase a ticket for Atlanta, please.

A : Did you make a reservation, sir?

P : No, I didn't.

A : When would you like to leave?

P : July 21st.

A : What class would you like?

P : Economy class.

A : Would you like a round-trip ticket or one way ticket?

P : One way ticket, please.

A : We have two seats available, one at 10 a.m. and another at 4 p.m. Which one would you like?

P : I'll take the 4 p.m. flight.

Useful Expressions

- ______ Airlines. ______ Speaking. May I help you?
- We have some seats available at ________.
- When do you want to *fly?*
  go
  leave
- *Would you like to book your return flight,* too*?*
  Do you want a return reservation
- What class would you like-economy, business or first?
- Any stopovers?
- May I have your *name and address,* please?
  credit card number
- Your reservation is confirmed for Asiana Flight OZ202 departing for L.A. on July 2 at 2 p.m.
  You'll have to reconfirm your reservation at least seventy-two hours before your departure.
  Please plan to arrive at the airport at least two hours prior to the departure time.
- Thank you for calling ___ Airlines.

3. Check-In(탑승 수속)

탑승 수속(Check-In)이란 공항에서 출국하기 위한 첫 번째 단계로, 손님이 좌석을 배정받고 수하물을 부친 후 탑승권을 받는 과정이다.

탑승 수속은 무인발권/탑승 수속기(Kiosk express check-in)를 이용하는 방법과 항공사 카운터를 이용하는 방법 등 두 가지가 있다. 먼저 무인발권/탑승 수속기를 이용하는 서비스는 승객이 공항에서 탑승 수속 카운터를 거치지 않고, 일정한 확인단계를 거친 후 스스로 항공권을 구매하거나 탑승권을 발급받는 것이다. 손님이 무인발권/탑승 수속기를 이용하면 당일 출발편의 예약, 발권, 좌석배정 및 탑승권 발급이 가능하며, 인터넷으로 항공권을 구매하고 좌석배정까지 마치고 공항에 나오는 경우에는 바로 탑승권을 교부받아 항공기를 탑승하러 갈 수 있어 더욱 빠르고 편리하게 여행할 수 있다.

두 번째로, 항공사 카운터를 이용한 탑승절차를 밟기 위해서는 손님은 항공사 직원에게 여권, 비자(필요한 국가일 경우), 항공권(혹은 e-티켓 확인증) 등을 제출하게 된다. 그러면 항공사 직원은 서류와 예약 여부를 확인한 뒤 좌석을 배정해 주는데, 이때 창가와 통로쪽, 좌석 중 손님이 원하는 좌석을 물어보고 좌석번호를 정해준다. 또 수하물의 무게를 달아보고 이상이 없으면 맡긴 짐에 수하물 물표를 달고 그 인환증을 항공표에 붙여 주는데, 이것은 도착지 공항에서 수하물을 찾을 때 필요하다. 이러한 절차가 끝나면 항공사 직원은 손님에게 이미 제출한 서류와 함께 탑승권을 주며 탑승구와 좌석번호를 확인시켜 준다.

일반적으로 수하물을 미국에서는 baggage, 영국에서는 luggage라고 한다. 수하물은 항공사의 카운터를 통해 보내는 것과 손님 자신이 비행기에 들고 들어가는 carry-on baggage로 나뉜다. 무료 수하물 허용량은 손님의 여정과 탑승하는 좌석 등급, 회원 등급에 따라 가져갈 수 있는 짐의 크기와 무게나 개수가 다르게 적용된다. 대한항공의 경우 1, 2등석 손님은 기내 무료 휴대수하물을 2개까지 허용하며, 그 짐들은 18kg(가로 55cm+세로 40cm+높이 20cm) 또는 가로+세로+높이 3면의 합이 115cm 이하여야 한다. 일반석은 기내 휴대수하물이 1개만 허용되나 추가적으로 노트북 컴퓨터, 서류가방이나 핸드백 중 1개에 한해 더 허용되며, 그것은 12kg(가로 55cm+세로 40cm+높이 20cm) 또는 가로+세로+높이 3면의 합이 115cm 이하여야 한다.

그러나 일부 품목들은 운송에 제한을 받을 수 있다. 다음과 같은 운송금지 품목은 기내 반입이나 수하물로 맡기는 것이 금지되어 있다: 페인트, 라이터용 연료와 같은 발화성/인화성 물질, 산소캔, 부탄가스캔 등 고압가스 용기, 총기, 폭죽 등 무기 및 폭발물류, 기타 탑승객 및 항공기에 위험을 줄 가능성이 있는 품목 등. 또한 모든 종류의 도검류, 골프채, 곤봉, 가위, 손톱깎이, 배터리 등과 같이 타 고객에게 위해를 가할 수 있는 품목의 경우 기내 반입은 제한을 받지만 위탁수하물로 탁송할 수 있다. 소량의 개인용 화장품 및 여행 중 필요한 의약품은 소량에 한하여 기내로 반입이 가능하다.

출입국 흐름도 Arrival and Departure Flow Diagram

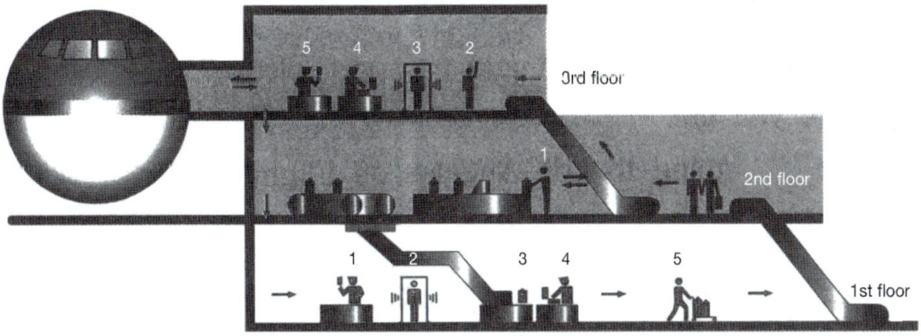

입국시 절차(Entry Procedures)	출국시 절차(Exit Procedures)
1. 입국 심사(Immigration Check)	1. 탑승 수속(Boarding Procedures)
⇩	⇩
2. 보안 검색(Security Check)	2. 출국 일반 대합실(Departure Waiting Area)
⇩	⇩
3. 수하물 회수(Baggage Retrieval)	3. 보안 검색(Security Check)
⇩	⇩
4. 세관 검사(Customs Clearance)	4. 휴대폰 검사(Carry-On-Check)
⇩	⇩
5. 입국 일반 대합실(Arrival Waiting Area)	5. 출국 심사(Emigration Check)

기본 어휘

airport tax	aisle	baggage	baggage claim check
breakable	briefcase	check in	non-smoking
passport	seat	smoking	ticket(booth)
window			

Dialogue 1

탑승 수속 1

A: Airline agent, P: Passenger

A : Good afternoon. What can I do for you, sir?

P : I want to check in, please.

A : May I see your ticket and passport, please?

P : Here you are.

A : Are you going to Los Angeles on Flight 002?

P : That's right.

A : Do you have any baggage to check?

P : Just one.

A : Anything breakable?

P : No.

A : Would you put your baggage on the scale, please?

P : O.K.

A : Window or aisle seat?

P : An aisle seat, please.

A : Here are your boarding pass and baggage claim check. Your seat is 37C aisle. You'll be boarding at Gate number 13. Be sure to be on time, 3:30 p.m.

Dialogue 2

탑승 수속 2

A: Airline agent, P: Passenger

A : Let me see your ticket, please.

P : Here it is. I would like an aisle seat, please.

A : O.K. How many pieces of baggage would you like to check?

P : Just one. I'll carry this briefcase myself.

(······)

A : All right, sir. Here's your boarding pass and this is your baggage claim check. Your seat number is 7-C. Boarding will begin at 10:30 a.m at Gate 12. Purchase an airport tax ticket at one of those ticket booths over there, please.

P : All right.

A : Thank you, sir. Enjoy your trip.

Dialogue 3

탑승 수속 3

A: Airline agent, P: Passenger

A : Hi.

P : (Putting his ticket and passport on the counter) Hi.

A : Window seat or aisle?

P : Aisle, please.

A : OK, sir. How many pieces of baggage would you like to check?

P : Two. I'll carry this briefcase myself.

A : All right, sir.

(······)

A : Here's your boarding pass and this is your baggage claim check. Boarding will be begin at 2:20 at Gate 14. Purchase an airport use fee ticket at one of those ticket booths over there, please.

P : All right.

A : Thank you, sir.

Dialogue 4 탑승 수속 4

A: Airline agent, P: Passenger

A : Let me see your ticket, please.

P : Here you are. I would like a window seat, please.

A : Sure. Here it is. Your seat number is 24-A.
Enjoy your trip, sir.

P : Thank you.

4. Security Check-In(보안 수속)

Dialogue

O: Officer, P: Passenger

O : Please put all carry-on luggage on the conveyor. Step right this way, sir.
(Beep)
Please empty your pockets and go through again, ma'am.
(Beep)
Please step this way, ma'am.

P : What was that buzz?

O : The metal detector has sensed a metal object on you. Please step back.
What do you have in this pocket?

P : Oh, sorry. Just some keys.

O : That's fine. Thank you, ma'am.
You can go through.

5. Reguest of connecting flight(연결편 문의)

Dialogue

A: Airline agent, P: Passenger

P : Can you help me?

A : Certainly. What can I do for you?

P : Our plane was late. I think we may have missed our connecting flight.

A : What is your flight?

P : Flight OZ 302 to Los Angeles.

A : You have not missed your flight. It is boarding now.

6. Reguest of boarding station(탑승구 문의)

Dialogue

A: Airline agent, P: Passenger

A : Excuse me. Can you direct me to Gate 8?

P : Sure. Go down the stairs right over there and you will see some directions.

P : Thank you.

A : Sure.

7. Pre-boarding station(탑승구 입구)

Dialogue

G: Gate agent, P: Passenger

P : Is this where I check in for Flight 052?

G : Yes, ma'am. May I see your boarding pass?

P : Yes, here it is.

G : Your seat is 37C, economy class. Boarding will start in a few minutes. Here is your boarding pass.

P : Thank you.

G : You're welcome.

NOTES:

Useful Expressions

- Good morning. What can I do for you?
- May I see your ticket and passport, please?
- Are you going to L.A. on Flight OZ202?
- Do you have any baggage to check?
- How many pieces of baggage would you like to check?
- Would you put your baggage on the scale, please?
- Window or aisle (seat)?
- Here are your boarding pass and baggage claim check. Your seat number is ______.
  Gate number is ____.
- Be sure to be on time.
- Please put all carry-on baggage on the conveyor.
  Step right this way, please.
- Please empty your pockets and go through again, sir.
- Enjoy your trip.

Chapter 02

Check-in Announcements
탑승 수속 관련 공항 내 안내방송

이 장은 공항에서 손님 탑승 전에 이루어지는 안내방송부분으로 여기에는 출국수속, 탑승 수속, 보안 수속, 출발편 지연 및 결항, 결항에 따른 재예약 및 탑승 안내방송 등이 포함되어 있다. 탑승 수속은 국제선의 경우 2시간 전, 국내선의 경우 1시간 전에 이루어지며, 보안수속은 비행기 출발 20~30분 전에 실시된다. 비행기가 결항된 경우에는 손님들의 편의를 위해 다른 비행기로 가실 수 있도록 빠른 시간 내에 재예약방송을 해줌으로써 결항에 따른 손님의 불만을 조금이나마 줄일 수 있다.

1. Announcement in the airport(공항 내 안내방송)

방송

① Flight CX 265 to Hong Kong due to depart at 10:30 will now leave at 11:00.

② Flight SQ 467 to Bangkok due to depart at 14:00 has been delayed until 15:30.

③ Flight KE 413 to Atlanta due to depart at 13:30, passengers please await further information.

④ Flight OZ 211 to Los Angeles due to depart at 10:00 is now boarding at Gate 8.

⑤ Passengers traveling on Fight CI 499 to Beijing, due to depart at 14:00, please go to the information desk.

⑥ Passenger, Mr. In-Soo Kim, please report to our staff at the desk at Gate 9. There is a message for you.

⑦ This is a staff announcement. Eun-A Lee please go to the information desk immediately. Eun-A Lee to the Information desk.

해설

① 10시 30분 출발 예정인 홍콩행 케세이 퍼시픽 항공 265편이 11시에 출발 할 것입니다.

② 14시에 출발 예정인 방콕행 싱가포르 항공 467편이 15:30분으로 지연되었습니다.

③ 13시 출발 예정인 애틀랜타행 대한항공 413편을 이용하실 손님 분들은 안내방송을 기다려 주십시오.

④ 10시 출발 예정인 로스앤젤레스행 아시아나항공 211편을 이용하실 손님들은 지금 8번 탑승구에서 탑승하시기 바랍니다.

⑤ 14시 출발 예정인 북경행 차이나항공 499편을 이용하실 손님께서는 안내 데스크로 가주십시오.

⑥ 김인수 씨께서는 9번 탑승구로 오셔서 메시지를 받아 가십시오.

⑦ 직원을 찾습니다. 이은아씨 지금 즉시 안내데스크로 와주시기 바랍니다. 이은아씨 안내데스크로 와주십시오.

2. Government formalities for departure(출국 수속)

방송

May I have your attention, please? Passengers who have not finished the formalities for departure are requested to come to the customs office immediately. Your forms must be completed and checked before you board the plane. We have airline employees available to assist you. Promptly complete this necessary part of your flight. Thank you.

해설

손님 여러분, 안내말씀 드리겠습니다. 출국수속을 끝내지 못한 분들은 즉시 세관사무실로 와주시면 감사하겠습니다. 해당 서류 양식은 탑승 전에, 완전한지 확인을 받으셔야 합니다. 손님을 도와드릴 저희 항공사요원이 있습니다. 여행에 필요한 이 단계를 신속히 끝내시기 바랍니다. 감사합니다.

3. Check-in(탑승 수속: 국제선 2시간 전, 국내선 1시간 전)

방송

May I have your attention, please? Passengers for Asiana Airlines Flight OZ 211 bound for Los Angeles departing at 10:30, please go through check-in and baggage check at Asiana check-in counter. Thank you.

해설

손님 여러분, 안내 말씀 드리겠습니다. 10시 30분 출발예정인 아시아나항공 로스앤젤레스행 OZ 211편 항공기에 탑승하실 손님께서는 항공권과 수하물을 가지고 수속카운터에 가셔서 좌석배정을 받으시고 짐을 부치시기 바랍니다. 감사합니다.

4. Security check-in(보안 수속: 출발 20~30분 전)

방송

May I have your attention, please? Passengers for Korean Airlines Flight KE 413 bound for Atlanta departing at 14:30, please have your travel card and passport ready and proceed to the departure lounge. Thank you.

해설

손님 여러분, 안내 말씀 드리겠습니다. 14시 30분 출발예정인 대한항공 애틀랜타행 KE 413편 항공기에 탑승하실 손님께서는 여행카드와 여권을 준비하셔서 출발 탑승구에서 보안수속을 받아 주시기 바랍니다. 감사합니다.

5. Final call for security check-in(보안 수속 마지막 호출: 출발 10분 전)

방송

May I have your attention, please? This is the final call for Cathay Pacific Airlines Flight CX 265 bound for Hong Kong departing at 11:30. All remaining passengers who have finished check-in at the counter, please get on board immediately through the security check in the departure lounge. Thank you.

This is the final call Flight CX 265 to Hong Kong. Any remaining passengers please proceed immediately to gate number 12 where the aircraft is about to depart.

해설 손님 여러분, 안내 말씀 드리겠습니다. 11시 30분 출발예정인 케세이퍼시픽항공 홍콩행 CX 265편 항공기에 탑승하실 손님에 대한 마지막 보안수속 안내방송입니다. 지금 곧 출발 탑승구에서 보안수속을 마치시고 탑승하여 주시기 바랍니다. 감사합니다.

안내말씀 드리겠습니다. 홍콩행 CX 265편의 마지막 안내방송입니다. 탑승 수속을 마친 손님께서는 모두 지금 즉시 12번 탑승구로 가 주시기 바랍니다.

6. Departure delayed(출발편 지연)

1) With new departure time(새로운 출발시간 확정 안내)

방송

May I have your attention, please? We are sorry to announce that Asiana Airlines Flight OZ 211 bound for Los Angeles departing at 12:20 will be delayed due to dense fog(heavy snow, heavy rain, strong winds). The new departure time will be 14:30 p.m. Thank you.

해설 손님 여러분, 안내 말씀 드리겠습니다. 12시 20분 출발예정인 아시아나항공 로스앤젤레스행 OZ 211편 항공기는 짙은 안개(폭설, 폭우, 강풍)로 인하여 정시로부터 2시간 10분 지연되어 14시 30분에 출발 예정이오니 이점 널리 양해하여 주시기 바랍니다. 감사합니다.

2) Without new arrival time(새로운 출발시간 미정 안내)

방송

May I have your attention, please? We are sorry to announce that Korean Airlines Flight KE 413 bound for Atlanta departing at 13:30 will be delayed due to dense fog(heavy snow, heavy rain, strong winds). Further information will be announced as soon as possible. Thank you.

해설 손님 여러분, 안내 말씀 드리겠습니다. 13시 30분 출발예정인 대한항공 애틀랜타행 KE 413편 항공기는 짙은 안개(폭설, 폭우, 강풍)로 인하여 예정시간보다 다소 지연될 예정이오니 이점 널리 양해하여 주시기 바랍니다. 정확한 출발시간은 빠른 시간 내에 알려드리겠습니다. 감사합니다.

7. Departure cancelled(출발편 결항)

방송

May I have your attention, please? We are sorry to announce that Cathay Pacific Airlines Flight CX 265 bound for Hong Kong departing at 11:20 has been cancelled due to dense fog(heavy snow, heavy rain, strong winds). Passengers who want to make a reservation for another flight, please come to the information counter. Thank you.

해설

손님 여러분, 안내 말씀 드리겠습니다. 11시 20분 출발예정인 케세이퍼시픽항공 홍콩행 CX 265편 항공기는 짙은 안개(폭설, 폭우, 강풍)로 인하여 운항이 취소되었사오니 이점 널리 양해하여 주시기 바랍니다. 대단히 죄송합니다만 다른 비행편을 예약하실 손님께서는 안내카운터로 와 주시면 감사하겠습니다.

8. Boarding(탑승)

방송

Boarding will take place according to the seat numbers shown on the boarding cards. You are asked to proceed through the gate until these numbers are called. Thank you.

Your attention, please. Asiana Airlines announces the departure of Flight OZ 211 for Los Angeles. Those with first-class tickets, small children, or needing assistance please board at this time. Our staff is ready to assist you. We will call for other passengers in a few minutes. Thank you for flying Asiana Airlines today.

Economy class passengers holding boarding cards with seat numbers between rows 35 and 50 are requested to board now.

해설

탑승은 손님들이 가지고 계신 탑승권의 좌석번호에 따라 시작될 것입니다. 손님 여러분의 좌석번호가 불려질 때 탑승해 주시기 바랍니다. 감사합니다.

손님 여러분, 안내 말씀 드리겠습니다. 아시아나항공 로스앤젤레스행 OZ 211편이 곧 출발하겠습니다. 일등석표나 어린이를 동반하신 손님과 도움이 필요하신 손님은 즉시 탑승하시기 바랍니다. 저희 항공사 요원들이 도와드리겠습니다. 다른 손님들은 다음 방송이 나갈 때까지 동안 잠시 기다려 주시면 감사하겠습니다. 오늘도 저희 아시아나항공을 이용해 주셔서 감사합니다.

좌석번호가 이코노미석 35번에서 50번인 손님께서는 지금 탑승해 주시기 바랍니다.

PART 02

BEFORE TAKE-OFF

419
NC4
Asiana Airlines

Chapter 03

Before Take-off Service English
손님 탑승~비행기 이륙 전 영어

1. Passenger boarding(손님 탑승)

탑승 수속이 끝나면 출발 약 30분전 손님탑승이 시작된다. 보통 퍼스트 클래스(first class) 손님, 비즈니스 클래스(busincss class) 손님, 어린아이를 동반한 손님, 도움을 필요로 하는 손님부터 탑승하게 되며, 이코노미 클래스(economy class) 손님들은 제일 나중에 항공기 뒤쪽 좌석번호부터 탑승하게 된다. 기내 입구에서 손님을 맞이하는 승무원은 손님들에게 밝은 미소와 포근한 환대의 모습을 보여 주어 손님들에게 산뜻한 첫인상을 보여주어야 한다. 왜냐하면 이러한 첫인상은 항공사의 이미지뿐만 아니라 손님의 나머지 여정을 보다 부드럽고 즐겁게 해주기 때문이다. 또한 승무원들은 장애자와 같이 도움을 필요로 하는 손님 혹은 여성 손님, 특히 어린아이나 짐을 가지고 탑승하는 손님들에게는 적극적으로 도와주는 노력을 아끼지 말아야 한다.

이 탑승시간에는 짧은 시간 내에 많은 손님들이 탑승하게 되므로 기내는 매우 복잡하기 쉽다. 그러므로 기내 승무원들은 손님들이 탑승하고 자리를 찾는데 신속한 동작으로 도움을 주어 이륙준비가 늦어지지 않도록 해야 한다.

기본 어휘

aisle	baggage(=luggage)		bag
bassinet	belongings	boarding pass	boarding station
cabin	cabin crew	diaper	formula
lavatory	passenger	seat belt	steward
stewardess	welcome to ABC Airlines		

1) At the boarding station(기내 입구)

Dialogue 1

환영인사 및 좌석안내 1

C: Cabin crew(Seward/Stewardess, P: Passenger

C : Good afternoon. Welcome to United Airlines.
May I see your boarding pass, please?

P : Yes, here you are.

C : Thank you. Your seat number is 50-E.
Please take the aisle to the right.

P : Thank you.

C : You're welcome. Have a nice flight.

Dialogue 2

환영인사 및 좌석안내 2

C: Cabin crew(Seward/Stewardess, P: Passenger

P : (Showing the boarding pass) Excuse me.
Where is my seat?

C : It's over there. Use the next aisle, please.

P : Thank you.

Dialogue 3

환영인사 및 좌석안내 3

C: Cabin crew(Seward/Stewardess, P: Passenger

C : Good morning.
May I see your boarding pass, please?

P : Yes. It's 45-A.

C : 45-A, your seat is in the back of the cabin on your right.

P : Thank you.

C : My pleasure. Have a good flight.

2) In the cabin(기내)

(1) 무거운 짐을 가진 손님

Dialogue

C: Cabin crew(Seward/Stewardess, P: Passenger

C : May I help you with your bags, ma'am?

P : Thank you.

C : You're welcome. May I help you find your seat?

P : Yes, please. It's 43-B.

C : All right This way, please.

(······)

Here you are. Have a nice flight.

(2) 어린이를 동반한 손님

Dialogue 1 좌석안내

C: Cabin crew(Seward/Stewardess, P: Passenger

C : May I help you with your belongings, ma'am?

P : Yes, please. Thank you.

C : My pleasure.

May I see your boarding pass, please?

P : Here it is.

C : Thank you. This way, please.

Here you are. These are your seats. Would you mind keeping your bags under the seat, please? That's a beautiful girl. She is so cute.

P : Thank you so much.

C : You're welcome. If you need anything during the flight, please let us know.

Dialogue 2

어린이 요람 서비스

C: Cabin crew(Seward/Stewardess, P: Passenger

C : Would you like a (baby) bassinet?

P : Yes, please.

C : Certainly, ma'am. I'll get one for you right after take-off for your baby's safety.

(······)

Here is your bassinet. We also have diapers, bottles, baby food and formula. If you need anything, please let us know. Have a nice flight, ma'am.

(3) 음료수 요청

Dialogue

C: Cabin crew(Seward/Stewardess, P: Passenger

P : Stewardess, can I have a glass of water?

C : Certainly, sir. I'll get it for you right away.

(……)

I'm sorry to have kept you waiting.

Here is your drink, sir.

(4) 좌석정리 요청

Dialogue

C: Cabin crew(Seward/Stewardess, P: Passenger

C : Excuse me, sir.

Would you mind taking your seat, please?

P : Oh, I'm sorry.

C : Thank you, sir. Have a pleasant flight.

(5) 이륙 전 화장실 사용

Dialogue

C: Cabin crew(Seward/Stewardess, P: Passenger

P : Can I use the lavatory now?

C : I'm sorry, sir. But would you mind using the lavatory after take-off?

P : I can't stand it.

C : All right, but please hurry. We'll be taking off soon.

Useful Expressions

- Good *morning, sir.* Welcome to *Asiana.*
  afternoon ma'am *Korean Airlines*
  evening *Northwest*
- May I see your boarding pass, please? Thank you.
- *You're welcome, sir.*
  = My pleasure, ma'am.
- It is in the *front* of the cabin *on the right.*
  middle *on the left*
  rear
- I'm sorry to have kept you waiting. This way, please.
- Thank you for waiting.
- Certainly, sir. I'll get it for you *as soon as possible.*
  right after take-off
- Would you mind *using the lavatory after take-off,* please?
  keeping your bag under your seat
- May I help you *with your bags,* ma'am?
  find your seat
- Here is your __________, sir.
- Would you please take your seat during boarding, sir?
- If you need anything during the flight, please let us know.
- Have a *pleasant* flight.
  good
  nice

2. Seating arrangements(좌석 배정)

손님이 기내에 들어서면 모든 승무원들은 각자의 위치에서 친절하고 명랑한 인사를 하여야 하며, 가능한 한 손님 개개인에게 인사를 하여야 한다. 외국인에게는 해당 국가어로 인사를 하도록 한다. 승무원들은 가능하면 손님 개개인의 좌석까지 안내를 해주며, 노인, 어린이, 환자 및 유아동반 손님의 탑승 시는 적극적으로 도와준다.

승무원은 각자의 위치를 중심으로 신속하고 유연성 있게 행동해야 하며, 문 쪽 등에서 승무원 상호간에 불필요한 잡담을 해서는 안 된다.

또한 일행이 있는 손님은 가능한 한 같이 앉을 수 있도록 배려해야 하며, 승무원의 편의를 위하여 손님의 좌석을 옮길 것을 무리하게 요구해서는 안 된다. 마지막으로 자기 좌석에서 벗어나 이곳 저곳으로 왔다갔다 하는 손님이 없도록 유의한다.

기본 어휘

arrange(ment)	assign	available	bother
change	double seating	empty	inconvenience
occupied			

1) Separated passengers(일행과 같은 좌석을 원하는 손님의 요청)

Dialogue 1 빈 좌석이 있을 경우 1

C: Cabin crew(Seward/Stewardess, P: Passenger

P : Stewardess, my friend and I were assigned separate seats. Do you have any empty seats together?

C : I see, sir. We have some empty seats in the middle of the cabin. Would that be alright, sir?

P : That's fine. Thank you.

C : This way, please.

(……)

Here you are. Have a nice flight, sir.

Dialogue 2 빈 좌석이 있을 경우 2

C: Cabin crew(Seward/Stewardess, P: Passenger

P : My wife is sitting over there, and we want to sit together.

C : I'll see if it can be arranged after take-off, sir.

(……)

Thank you for waiting. There are empty seats in the back of the cabin. Would that be alright, sir?

P : Yes, that'll be fine. Thank you.

C : You're welcome. This way, please.

(……)

Here are your seats. Have a nice flight, sir.

Dialogue 3 빈 좌석이 없을 경우

C: Cabin crew(Seward/Stewardess, P1, P2: Passenger

P1 : My wife is sitting over there, and we want to sit together. Is that possible?

C : I'll see if it can be arranged, sir.

After take-off, I'll come back and let you know.

(……)

I'm sorry, sir, but all the seats are occupied.

Where is your wife sitting?

P1 : Just across the aisle there.

C : Just a moment, please.

(Go to P2 to ask changing seats)

C : Excuse me, sir. I'm sorry to bother you. But we have a couple who has been assigned separate seats. Would you mind changing seats so they can sit together?

P2 : No, I don't. Where should I sit?

C : Thank you very much, sir. This way, please.

(……)

I'm sorry for the inconvenience, sir.

Would you care for something to drink?

P2 : No, thank you.

C : Sir, this gentleman is willing to change seats with you. This way, please.

(……)

Here you are, sir.

P1 : Thank you. I appreciate it.

C : My pleasure, sir. Have a nice flight.

2) Changing seats(손님의 좌석 변경 요청)

Dialogue 1

빈 좌석이 있을 경우 1

C: Cabin crew(Seward/Stewardess, P: Passenger

P : Excuse me, may I change my seat?

C : Yes, you may.

We have lots of empty seats at the back.

P : I'd like a window seat.

C : Please, come this way, sir.

Dialogue 2

빈 좌석이 있을 경우 2

C: Cabin crew(Seward/Stewardess, P: Passenger

P : Do you have empty seats in the front of the cabin?

C : Just a moment, please. I'll see what's available.

(……)

We have empty seats in the middle of the cabin. Would that be alright, sir?

P : Yes, that'll be fine.

C : This way, please.

(……)

Here you are. Have a nice flight, sir.

Dialogue 3

빈 좌석이 없을 경우

C: Cabin crew(Seward/Stewardess, P: Passenger

P : Stewardess. I want to change seats.

C : Where would you like to sit, sir?

P : In the front, if possible.

C : I'll see if it can be changed, sir.

(……)

Thank you for waiting. I'm sorry, but I'm afraid all the seats in the front are occupied.

Would you care for something to drink, sir?

P : No, thank you.

C : If you need anything during the flight, please let me know.

3) Wrong seats(손님이 잘못된 좌석에 앉음)

Dialogue

C: Cabin crew(Seward/Stewardess, P1, P2: Passenger

P1 : Excuse me, stewardess. I think this is my seat.

C : (To P1) Excuse me, sir. May I see your boarding pass, please? Thank you.

(To P2) Excuse me, sir. May I see your boarding pass, please? I'm sorry, but I'm afraid you're in the wrong seat. Your seat is behind this one, sir. Would you mind changing seats, please?

P2 : Sure. Where is my seat?

C : (To P1) It is this one, sir.

Have a pleasant flight. (……)

(To P2) This way, please.

Your seat is right here, sir. I'm sorry for the inconvenience.

Have a nice flight, sir.

4) Double seating(이중좌석 발생)

Dialogue

C: Cabin crew(Seward/Stewardess, P1, P2: Passenger

P1 : Stewardess, this passenger is in my seat.

C : May I see your boarding pass, please? Thank you. I'm sorry, but I'm afraid there has been a mistake in seating arrangements.

(To P2) This way, please. Would you mind waiting here, sir? I'll check it for you immediately.

(……)

Thank you for waiting. Your seat is arranged, sir. It's 42H. This way, please.

(……)

I'm sorry for the inconvenience, sir.

Would you care for something to drink, sir?

Useful Expressions

- Your seat is *behind this one.*
  three rows in front of this seat
- Would you *mind changing* seats, sir?
  care to change
- *Please come this way,* please.
  This way
- I'm sorry, but I'm afraid *you're in the wrong seat.*
  all the seats in the front are occupied
  there has been a mistake in seating arrangements
- I am sorry, ma'am, but all the seats are occupied.
- I'm sorry *for the inconvenience,* sir.
  to bother you
- We have some seats in the *front* of the cabin.
  middle
  back
- I'll see if it can be arranged.
- I'll check it for you immediately.
- It is a smoking zone. Would that be alright, sir?

3. Carry-on baggage(기내 휴대품)

승무원들은 손님들에게 소지한 짐을 좌석 아래나 선반 위에 올려놓도록 여쭤야 한다. 만일 좌석 아래나 선반 위에 공간이 없다면 손님들에게 양해를 구한 다음 짐을 받아 기내 뒤쪽에 보관할 수도 있다. 특별히 무겁거나 깨지기 쉬운 물건들은 선반 위나 손님들이 잘 다니는 곳에 보관해서는 안 된다. 만일 손님들이 좌석을 바꾼다면 짐을 옮기지 않도록 양해를 구해야 하며, 승무원 편리를 위해 손님들에게 어떤 일을 하도록 요구해서는 안 된다.

통로는 항상 뜻하지 않은 비상상황과 손님의 편리를 위하여 항시 열려 있어야 한다(open).

기본 어휘

carry-on baggage		coat room	fall out
hang	landing	relax	overhead bin(rack)
seat belt	sign	take-off	

1) Baggage in the aisle(통로의 짐)

Dialogue 1 통로의 짐 1

C: Cabin crew(Seward/Stewardess, P: Passenger

C : Excuse me, sir. Is this bag yours?

P : Yes, it is.

C : I'm sorry, sir, but we have to keep the aisle open(or clear). Would you mind keeping your bag under your seat, please?

P : Sure.

C : Thank you. Have a nice flight.

Dialogue 2 통로의 짐 2

C: Cabin crew(Seward/Stewardess, P: Passenger

P : Excuse me, stewardess. Where can I put my bag? It doesn't fit under my seat and the overhead bin is full.

C : Would you like me to keep your bag in the back of the cabin?

P : Yes. Would you do that? Thank you.

C : My pleasure. Have a pleasant flight.

2) Baggage on the seat(좌석 위의 짐)

Dialogue

C: Cabin crew(Seward/Stewardess, P: Passenger

C : Excuse me, ma'am. We will be taking off shortly. That may fall during take-off. Would you mind keeping your bag under your seat, please?

P : No problem.

3) Baggage in the overhead bin(선반의 짐)

Dialogue

C: Cabin crew(Seward/Stewardess, P: Passenger

P : (putting a heavy bag in the overhead bin)

C : Excuse me, sir. Would you mind keeping your bag under your seat, please?

It might fall out during the flight.

(……)

That's perfect. Thank you, sir.
Have a nice flight.

4) Carry-on baggage and coats(기내 휴대품과 코트)

Dialogue 1 기내 휴대품

C: Cabin crew(Seward/Stewardess, P: Passenger

C : Would you like me to keep your bag in the back of the cabin, ma'am?

P : No, that's alright. I'll keep it here.

C : Certainly, ma'am. Have a pleasant flight.

Dialogue 2 코 트

C: Cabin crew(Seward/Stewardess, P: Passenger

C : Excuse me, ma'am. Would you like me to hang your coat(jacket) in the coat room?

P : Yes, thank you.

C : You're welcome, ma'am. Have a nice flight.

Useful Expressions

- I'm sorry, sir, but we have to keep the aisle open.
- We are going to take off soon.
- Would you mind keeping your bag under your seat, please?
- It might fall out during the flight.
- Would you like me to *keep* your *coat* in the *coat room, ma'am?*
  put *bag* *back of the cabin*
- I'll be glad to keep it for you in the *coat room.*
  back of the cabin

NOTES:

4. Smoking and No Smoking(흡연과 금연)

많은 손님들은 담배 연기나 흡연 손님들에 대해 민감한 반응을 보인다. 이러한 이유와 깨끗한 환경에 대한 사회적인 시각에 발맞춰 많은 항공사들이 기내에서의 철저한 금연을 실시하고 있다.

또한 기내 화장실에서의 흡연은 안전상의 이유로 금지되어 있다. 비행기가 정지 혹은 이·착륙시 모든 손님들은 금연을 하도록 요구받는다. 만일 어떤 손님이 흡연을 하고 있다면 손님의 기분이 나쁘지 않도록 조심스럽고도 정중하게 금연에 대한 양해를 구하도록 한다.

airsick	allowed	cigar/pipe	cigarette
lavatory	no smoking zone	prohibited	put out
safety	smoking sign(zone)		

1) Smoking before take-off(이륙 전 흡연)

Dialogue

C: Cabin crew(Seward/Stewardess, P: Passenger

P : (smoking)

C : Excuse me, sir. Would you mind putting out your cigarette, please? The smoking sign is on, sir.

P : Sure.

C : Thank you. Have a nice flight.

2) Smoking in the lavatory(화장실에서의 흡연)

Dialogue

C: Cabin crew(Seward/Stewardess, P: Passenger

C : Excuse me, sir. Would you mind putting out your cigarette before using the lavatory, please?
Smoking in the lavatory is prohibited, sir.

P : Why?

C : It's for your safety, sir. Thank you.

Useful Expressions

- The non-smoking sign is on.
  Would you mind putting out your cigarette, please?
- Smoking cigar is not allowed in the cabin.
- Smoking in the lavatory is not allowed, sir.

NOTES:

5. Preparation for take-off(이륙 준비)

모든 손님이 탑승을 하면 기내 승무원들은 이륙 준비를 위해 각 손님들을 체크하느라 바빠지게 된다. 비행기문이 잠기면 승무원들은 비행기 이륙까지 많은 시간이 남지 않게 된다. 비행기가 활주로로 이동하게 되면 한 명의 스튜어디스는 환영인사 방송을 하게 되며, 다른 승무원들은 손님들에게 신문을 나눠드리게 된다.

환영인사에 이어 손님들에게 비상사태에 대비한 행동요령, 즉 산소마스크 사용, 구명조끼 착용법 등의 시범을 보여준다. 이렇게 짧은 시간동안 기내 승무원들은 비행기 이륙 전 기내손님과 자기들이 앉는 자리를 체크하게 된다. 기내 체크동안 "금연과 안전벨트 착용" 신호등이 켜지고, 모든 손님들은 자신들의 자리로 되돌아가 자기 앞의 식사 테이블(tray table)과 뒤로 젖혔던 좌석도 원위치로 가도록 한다. 만일 손님들의 안전벨트가 느슨하거나 제대로 착용되지 않았다면 승무원은 손님의 안전벨트 착용을 도와주며, 특히 유아 또는 어린이의 안전벨트를 철저히 체크해야 한다.

기내 체크가 끝나고 비행기가 관제탑의 이륙허가를 기다리며 활주로에 대기하고 있는 동안 승무원들은 자신의 자리로 이동하여 안전벨트를 착용한다.

기본 어휘

close	fasten	fold	magazine
newspaper	pillow	recline	return
run out of	seat back	tray table	upright

1) Seat belt(안전벨트)

Dialogue 1 안전벨트 착용 확인

C: Cabin crew(Seward/Stewardess, P: Passenger

P : (seat belt not fastened)

C : Excuse me, sir. Would you mind fastening your seat belt, please? We will be taking off shortly. Thank you. Have a pleasant flight.

Dialogue 2

안전벨트 착용을 원하지 않는 손님의 경우

C: Cabin crew(Seward/Stewardess, P: Passenger

C : Excuse me, sir.
Would you mind fastening your seat belt, please?

P : I don't like fastening the seat belt.
Don't worry, stewardess.

C : I'm sorry, sir. But I must ask you to fasten your seat belt before take-off.
It's for your own safety, sir.

Dialogue 3

안전벨트 착용법을 모르는 손님의 경우

C: Cabin crew(Seward/Stewardess, P: Passenger

P : Excuse me.
Will you show me how to fasten my seat belt?

C : Of course, sir. Pull it this way.
If you need any help, just push this call button.

P : Thank you.

C : You're welcome.

Dialogue 4

좌석 원위치

C: Cabin crew(Seward/Stewardess, P: Passenger

C : Please fasten your seat belt.

P : (Fasten the seat belt.)

C : Put your seat back up, please.

P : Is this all right?

C : Sure. Please put your bag under the seat in front of you.

2) Tray table/Seat back(트레이 테이블 및 좌석 원위치)

Dialogue 1 트레이 테이블 원위치

C: Cabin crew(Seward/Stewardess, P: Passenger

C : Excuse me, ma'am. Would you mind closing(or folding) your tray table (for take-off), please?

P : O.K.

C : Thank you, ma'am.

Dialogue 2 좌석 원위치

C: Cabin crew(Seward/Stewardess, P: Passenger

C : Excuse me, sir. Would you mind returning your seat back to the upright position for take-off, please?

P : O.K.

C : Thank you, sir.

3) Newspaper service(신문 서비스)

Dialogue 1 신문 서비스 1

C: Cabin crew(Seward/Stewardess, P: Passenger

C : Would you like to read a newspaper, sir?

P : I want this one.

Dialogue 2

신문 서비스 2

C: Cabin crew(Seward/Stewardess, P: Passenger

C : Would you like a newspaper or a magazine, sir?

P : Yes. Do you have the Dong-A Daily?

C : Yes, here you are.

P : Thank you.

C : You're welcome.

Dialogue 3

손님의 신문요청

C: Cabin crew(Seward/Stewardess, P: Passenger

P : Can I have a Sports-Chosun?

C : I'm sorry, but I'm afraid we have run out of the Sports-Chosun. Would you care for Dong-A Daily, instead?

P : Oh, that's fine.

C : Here is your newspaper, sir. Have a nice flight, sir.

Useful Expressions

- Would you mind *fastening your seat belt,* please?
  closing your tray table
  returning your seat back
  to the upright position

- We will be taking off shortly.
- Would you *like* *a newspaper,* sir?
  care for *a TIME magazine*

- Here is the newspaper you requested, sir.

- We have run out of them. (or)
  We don't have it on board.

NOTES:

Chapter 04

Before Take-off Announcements

이륙 준비과정 기내 안내방송

이 장은 손님이 탑승을 하면서 비행기가 이륙하기까지의 과정에서 발생하는 안내방송 부분으로 여기에는 탑승 비행기편에 대한 소개, 환영인사, 비상사태 안전시범, 이륙 및 전자기기 사용제한 안내방송 등이 포함된다.

기내방송 서비스는 손님에 대한 가장 직접적이고 효과적인 서비스 수단 중의 하나이며, 또한 회사를 대표하는 중요한 역할을 담당하므로 정확하게 전달하여야 된다. 또한 객실승무원들은 손님들이 협소한 좌석과 통행에 불편한 복도에서 장시간 단조롭게 여행해야 하므로 항공여행을 한정된 공간에서의 부자유스런 여행으로 인식하기 쉽다는 점을 고려하여 기내 방송시 기지와 재치, 신속한 상황판단 및 융통성을 발휘하여야 한다.

기내 방송시의 일반적인 유의사항은 다음과 같다.

① 항공기별로 마이크 감도 및 음량이 다르므로 비행 전에(pre-flight check) 마이크 상태를 점검한다.

② 방송시 마이크의 음량은 대체로 대화하는 수준이거나 또는 그보다 다소 낮은 목소리로 명료하게 방송한다.

③ 발음은 정확히 하고, 쉴 곳과 강조해야 할 부분을 구분하여 방송한다.

④ 마이크를 통해 숨소리나 바람소리가 송신되지 않도록 해야 한다.

⑤ 갑자기 큰소리로 방송하여 손님을 놀라게 하지 말아야 한다.

⑥ 정형적인(routine) 방송문을 기본으로 하여 최대한의 신선미를 가미한 자율적인 방송을 하되, 너무 길어서는 안되며, 예의에 벗어나거나 촌스러운 문구는 피하도록 한다.

⑦ 콧소리를 내거나 발음과 억양에 있어 반복적이거나 끝을 늘리는 등의 멋을 부리는 방송은 금한다.

⑧ '악천후', '엔진이상', '번개', '계기이상' 등의 용어는 절대 사용해서는 안 된다.

⑨ 탑승편 안내와 환영인사(welcome) 방송에서 긴 인사말이 서로 중복되지 않도록 한다.

1. Boarding(탑승: 80% 완료 시점)

방송

Good morning(afternoon, evening) ladies and gentlemen. This is Korean Airlines KE 317 bound for Chicago.

All heavy or fragile items must be placed under your seat, and be careful when you open the overhead bin to prevent items inside from falling out. Thank you for your cooperation.

해설

손님 여러분, 안녕하십니까? 저희 비행기는 시카고까지 가는 대한항공 KE 317편입니다.

손님 여러분의 안전을 위해 깨지기 쉬운 물건 등은 좌석 밑에 놓아주시고, 선반을 여실 때는 안에 있는 물건이 떨어질 우려가 있으니 주의하여 주시기 바랍니다.

2. Take-off delayed(이륙 지연)

1) Example 1(예 1)

방송

Ladies and gentlemen. Because of the current weather conditions at Incheon International Airport, our departure is going to be delayed about 30 minutes. We'll take off as soon as possible. Thank you.

해설 안내말씀 드리겠습니다. 인천국제공항의 날씨관계로 출발이 지연되고 있습니다. 약 30분 정도 지연될 것으로 예상됩니다만, 이륙 승인이 나는 대로 출발하겠습니다. 감사합니다.

2) Example 2(예 2)

방송

Ladies and gentlemen. The weather condition at Pusan airport have not improved yet. The decision will be made following the 11 o'clock weather check. Thank you for your understanding and patience.

해설 안내말씀 드리겠습니다. 공항의 기상이 호전되지 않고 있습니다. 11시 기상상황이 통보되는 대로 다시 출발 여부를 말씀드리겠습니다. 감사합니다.

3. Welcome(환영인사)

1) Example 1(예 1)

방송

Ladies and gentlemen, welcome aboard Asiana Airlines flight OZ 333 bound for Beijing.

Today's flight time will be about 2 hours 10 minutes following take-off. The captain of this flight is Eun-soo Park and this is your flight attendant Chang-uk Lee.

Now, please make sure that your seatback is in the upright position, your tray table is closed and your seatbelt is fastened. And we recommend that you continue to fasten your seatbelt while seated during the flight.

Also, refrain from using any electronic devices during take-off and landing for safety reasons. Your cooperation will be much appreciated.

If there is anything we can do for you, please let us know. We wish you a pleasant flight. Thank you.

승객 여러분들의 보다 편리하고 즐거운 여행을 위하여 다양한 종류의 비행 관련 정보를 안내하고 있습니다. 비행 속도, 고도, 현재 위치, 목적지까지의 거리와 남은 시간, 현지 시각 및 외부 온도 등 각종 운항 정보를 최신 컴퓨터 그래픽으로 기내 스크린을 통하여 제공해 드립니다.

(B747-400, B747-300 기종의 모든 항공기에 운영 중에 있습니다.

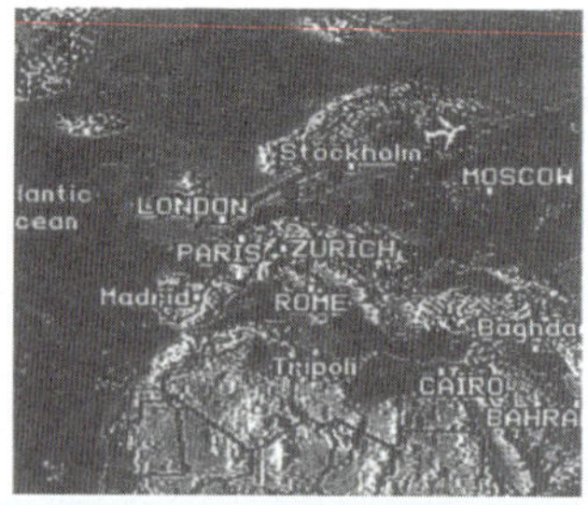

To make your travel more convenient and enjoyable, Air Show, an onboard information system, displays a variety of flight-related data on screen which include ground speed, altitude, time/ distance to destination, out side air temperature etc. (Available on all B747-400, B747-300 aircrafts.)

해설

손님 여러분, 안녕하십니까? 오늘 북경까지 가는 아시아나항공 OZ 333편을 이용해 주셔서 대단히 감사합니다. 오늘 비행시간은 이륙 후 2시간 10분이 소요될 예정입니다. 이 비행기의 기장은 박은수이며, 저는 승무원 이창욱입니다.

지금부터 좌석을 바로 해주시고, 좌석벨트를 매주십시오. 또한 여러분의 안전을 위해 좌석에 앉아 계시는 동안에는 좌석벨트를 가볍게 매고 계시기 바랍니다.

또한 항공기의 안전운항을 위해, 이·착륙 시에는 모든 전자제품의 사용이 금지되어 있사오니, 전원을 꺼 주시기 바랍니다.

목적지까지 즐겁고 안락한 여행이 되시도록 저희 승무원들은 정성을 다하겠습니다. 감사합니다.

2) Example 2(예 2)

방송

Good morning, ladies and gentlemen. Welcome aboard Korean Airlines Flight KE 653 bound for Bangkok. Commanding your plane this morning is Captain, Eun-soo Park. I'm Chief Purser, Chang-uk Lee. Please fasten your seat belt, return your seat to the upright position, and observe the no-smoking sign until it is turned off.

Also, refrain from using any electronic devices during take-off and landing for safety reasons.

We are waiting for clearance from the air traffic control tower. We expect to take off in a few minutes. If there is anything we can do for you, please let us know. Thank you.

해설 손님 여러분, 안녕하십니까? 방콕행 대한항공 KE 653편에 탑승해 주신 것을 환영합니다. 오늘 아침 여러분들의 비행기를 조정 하실 분은 기장 박은수입니다. 저는 기내 사무장 이창욱입니다. 좌석벨트를 메어 주시고 좌석을 바로 세워 주십시오. 그리고 금연 사인이 꺼질 때까지 금연을 지켜 주십시오. 또한 항공기의 안전을 위해, 이·착륙 시에는 모든 전자제품의 사용이 금지되어 있사오니, 전원을 꺼 주시기 바랍니다.

지금 저희 비행기는 관제탑으로부터 이륙허가를 기다리고 있습니다. 이륙허가가 나는 대로 곧 이륙하겠습니다. 비행동안 불편한 점이 있으시면 저희에게 말씀해 주십시오. 목적지까지 즐겁고 안락한 여행이 되시도록 손님 여러분을 정성을 다해 모시겠습니다. 감사합니다.

4. Safety demonstration(비상사태 안전시범)

1) Video(비디오)

방송 Ladies and gentlemen, we would like to familiarize you with the safety features of this craft. Please pay attention to the following video demonstration. Thank you.

해설 손님 여러분, 지금부터 비행 중 안전사항에 관한 비디오상영이 있겠습니다. 안전한 여행을 위해 주의를 기울여 주시기 바랍니다. 감사합니다.

2) Demonstration(시범)

방송

Ladies and gentlemen, we would like to inform you of the safety features of this aircraft.

1 In the case of emergency evacuation, there are emergency exits on both sides of the aircraft. In an emergency situation, emergency lights located in the ceiling and aisles will be turned on automatically to guide you to the exits. Please take a moment to identify the nearest exit from your seat.

2 To fasten your seat belt, please insert the metal tongue into the buckle and tighten the belt by pulling the loose end. To release your seat belt, lift up the metal cover.

3 If cabin pressure is interrupted for any reason, an overhead panel will be opened automatically, exposing several oxygen masks.
When your mask appears, pull the mask toward you and cover your nose and mouth with the mask. Then adjust the headband to fit your head.

4 In preparation for ditching, a life vest is located under your seat.
To put the vest on, slip it over your head. Take the strap and put it around your waist, then fasten. Tighten your vest by pulling the strap.
Your life vest can be inflated by pulling down on the two red knobs or by blowing into the inflation tubes on either side.
But, please do not inflate the vest while inside the aircraft.

5 Now please take a moment to review the safety features by looking through the safety instruction card located in your seat pocket. Thank you.

해설

손님 여러분, 이 비행기의 비상용 장비와 비상구 이용방법에 대해 말씀드리겠습니다.

1 비상탈출을 해야 할 경우, 여러분께서 사용할 비상구는 저희 승무원들이 가리키는 바와 같이 좌우에 각각 있습니다. 비상착륙을 했을 때는 모든 불이 꺼지는 수가 있으며, 이때는 자동적으로 복도와 선반 위에서 자동적으로 켜지는 비상등을 따라 탈출해 주십시오. 참고로, 여러분의 좌석에서 가장 가까운 비상구 위치를 확인하시기 바랍니다.

2 지금부터 좌석벨트를 매셨는지 확인해 주십시오. 벨트는 먼저 양쪽고리를 끼우신 다음, 몸에 맞도록 조여 주시고, 풀 때는 위 뚜껑을 들어 당겨 주십시오.

3 비행기의 여압장치 이상으로 인해 기내에 산소공급이 필요할 때는 머리 위 선반 속에 있는 산소마스크가 자동적으로 내려옵니다.

이때는 마스크를 앞으로 잡아당겨 호흡을 몇 번 하신 다음, 끈을 머리에 맞게 조여 주십시오.

4 지금 보시는 것은 좌석 밑에 있는 구명복이며, 바다에 내렸을 경우 사용하도록 준비되어 있습니다.

구명복을 착용하실 때는 머리 위에서부터 입으시고 끈을 허리에 감으신 다음, 앞에 있는 고리에 끼워 조여 주십시오.

앞에 있는 손잡이를 당기시면 부풀어지며, 충분히 부풀지 않을 때는 고무관을 불어 주십시오. 그러나 기내에서는 부풀리지 않도록 유의해 주십시오.

5 좌석 앞 주머니 속에 있는 비상장비와 비상탈출에 관한 자세한 사용 안내서를 반드시 읽고 참고하시기 바랍니다. 감사합니다.

5. Take-off(이륙)

방송

Ladies and gentlemen, we will be taking off shortly. Please make sure that your seat belt is fastened. Thank you.

해설

손님 여러분, 저희 비행기는 이륙하겠습니다. 좌석벨트를 매셨는지 다시 한번 확인해 주시기 바랍니다. 감사합니다.

6. Restriction on using electronic devices(전자기기 사용제한)

방송

Ladies and gentlemen, you may now use your electronic devices, but please refrain from using portable phones, televisions, pagers, wireless electronic games and toys, and any other type of radio or communication devices during the flight.

For further information, please contact your flight attendant. Thank you.

해설

손님 여러분, 저희 비행기는 현재 순항고도에 진입하고 있습니다. 지금부터는 전자제품의 사용이 가능합니다만, 특히 휴대용 전화기, TV, 무선 호출기, 각종 라디오, 장난감 작동 송수신기 등의 사용은 비행 중 계속해서 금지되오니, 손님 여러분들의 넓으신 양해 부탁드립니다.

좀더 아시고자 하는 내용이 있으시면 저희 승무원에게 문의해 주십시오. 자세히 안내해 드리겠습니다. 감사합니다.

PART 03

EN-ROUTE

Chapter 5 En-route Service English
Chapter 6 En-route Announcements

health tips for you flight 기내 건강 클리닉

A long trip on an airplane can be very tiring. Muscles may get tense and joints stiff from hours of sitting in the same position. Such fatigue and discomfort can be overcome with just a few, simple exercises. When the trip starts to get you down, take a deep breath, relax, and try the following.

장시간 앉아 여행하면서 몰려드는 피로감. 이러한 피로감은 간단한 체조로 극복할 수 있다. 자세를 바르게 하고 심호흡을 한 다음 편안한 마음으로 다음에 나오는 체조를 해 보자.

1. Knee Exercise 무릎 운동

Bend forward slightly, take your left knee in both hands, and pull it up towards your chest as far as you can. Hold that position for 10 to 15 seconds, and then slowly lower your knee to its original position. Repeat with the right knee.

몸을 앞으로 약간 구부린 다음 왼쪽 무릎을 양손으로 감싸고 가슴까지 끌어올린다. 약 10-15초 동안 그 상태를 계속 유지하다가 천천히 무릎을 아래로 내린다. 오른쪽 무릎도 같은 방법으로 반복한다.

2. Torso Exercise 상체 운동

Place your back flush against the back of your seat; then slowly bend your upper body forward, allowing your arms to hang loosely down to your ankles. After a moment, return to your upright position.

허리를 의자에 바짝 붙인 다음 서서히 상체를 앞으로 구부린다. 이 때 두 손은 자연스럽게 발목 쪽으로 향하게 하고 잠시후 다시 원위치로 돌아온다.

3. Elbow Stretching 팔꿈치 펴기 운동

Stretch both arms high over your head. With one hand grab the other wrist and gently pull in one direction. Repeat at 15 second intervals, changing directions each time.

양팔을 머리 위로 높이 들고 한 손으로 다른 팔의 손목을 잡는다. 그런 다음 부드럽게 잡아당긴다. 방향을 바꿔 15초 간격으로 반복한다.

4. Neck Exercise 목 운동

Completely relax your shoulders and allow your head to droop forward slowly. Slowly rotate your neck counterclockwise and then clockwise without applying any tension to the neck muscles.

어깨 힘을 쭉 뺀 후 천천히 고개를 숙인다. 목을 옆으로 편하게 눕힌 다음 좌우로 서서히 돌린다.

5. Shoulder Exercise 어깨 운동

Gently but firmly bring your shoulders forward and inward. Repeat this movement in the upward direction and then backward, finishing the exercise by pulling the shoulders downward.

어깨를 앞으로 둥글게 구부린다. 같은 동작을 위로 한 번, 뒤로 한 번씩 한다. 마지막으로 어깨를 아래로 떨어뜨린다. 각 동작을 부드럽게 연결시켜 운동한다.

Chapter 05

En-route Service English

기내 서비스영어

1. Earphone and Towel service(이어폰과 물수건 서비스)

기장이 환영인사, 비행 고도 및 속도, 날씨 상태 등을 방송할 때 승무원들은 손님에게 음료와 식사를 제공하기 위한 준비를 하게 된다. 식사를 위한 타월 서비스가 이루어지기 전 이어폰세트(earphone sets)가 기내 음악프로그램과 영화상영을 위해 손님들에게 나누어진다. 국제선의 경우 손님에게 이어폰 제공은 무료이나 몇몇 외국 항공사의 경우 얼마간의 사용료를 손님으로부터 받기도 한다. 이어폰 서비스가 끝나면 승무원들이 앞치마를 두른 채 기내 앞쪽으로부터 타월을 손님들에게 나눠준다.

기본 어휘

breakfast	compliments	disturb	earphone set
finished(with)	free of charge	pamphlet	presentation
refreshing	towel		

1) Hot towel service(물수건 서비스)

Dialogue 1 타월 제공

C: Cabin crew(Seward/Stewardess, P: Passenger

C : Please be careful. It's very hot, sir.

P : Thank you.

Dialogue 2 타월 수거

C: Cabin crew(Seward/Stewardess, P: Passenger

C : Excuse me, sir. Have you finished with your towel?

P : Yes, thank you.

C : (taking towel) You're welcome, sir.

Dialogue 3 잠자는 손님의 경우

C: Cabin crew(Seward/Stewardess, P: Sleeping Passenger

C : Excuse me, sir. Would you care for a hot towel?
We'll be serving dinner soon.

P : Oh, I see.

2) Earphone service(이어폰 서비스)

Dialogue 1 이어폰 제공 1

C: Cabin crew(Seward/Stewardess, P: Passenger

C : Excuse me, sir. Here's your earphone set.

P : No, thank you.

C : Are you sure? It's free of charge.

Dialogue 2

이어폰 제공 2

C: Cabin crew(Seward/Stewardess, P: Passenger

C : Would you care for an earphone set, ma'am?

P : Do you charge for it?

C : No, ma'am. It's free of charge.

P : Alright, I'll have one. Thank you.

C : You're welcome, ma'am.

Useful Expressions

- Would you care for a towel, sir?
- Please be careful. It's very hot, sir.
- Excuse me. Have you finished with your towel, sir?
- Would you care for a towel, sir?
- Please be careful. It's very hot, sir.
- Excuse me. Have you finished with your towel, sir?
- May I take your towel, sir?
- We'll be serving *dinner soon.*
  breakfast shortly

2. Meal and beverage service(식음료 서비스)

승무원들이 타월을 회수한 뒤에는 손님들은 다과(refreshments)와 식사가 제공된다는 방송을 듣게 된다. 퍼스트 클래스와 비즈니스 클래스의 손님들은 높은 품질의 음식과 다양한 음료 및 칵테일을 제공받게 되며, 이코노미 클래스 손님은 통상 2가지의 음식 중 1가지를 선택하게 된다. 손님들은 자기가 원하는 만큼의 음료를 무료로 제공받을 수 있으나 몇몇 항공사들은 와인, 맥주 등의 최소한의 돈을 내게 하기도 한다. 기내 승무원들은 칵테일을 만드는 법과 모든 주요리(entrees)에 대한 지식을 숙지하고 있어야 하고, 또한 손님들로부터 요구사항을 처리하기 위해 영어실력을 배양해야 한다.

식사 제공 때는 창가 좌석으로부터 중간석, 복도좌석의 순으로 서비스하며, 절대로 음식 트레이(entree tray)를 다른 손님을 통해 제공한다든가 손님의 머리 위로 전달하지 말아야 하며, 가능한 한 여자 손님 우선 순위로 서비스한다.

또한 일부 손님들은 특별한 기내식을 요구하기도 한다. 여기에는 야채식, 식사 조절식, 종교식, 영유아식 & 아동식, 기타 특별식 등이 있다.

첫째, 야채식의 종류는 다음의 표와 같다.

	육류	유제품	계란	뿌리채소
서양 채식	×	○	○	○
엄격한 서양 채식	×	×	×	○
인도 채식	×	○	×	○
엄격한 인도 채식	×	×	×	×
동양 채식	×	×	×	○

둘째, 식사 조절식은 건강상의 이유로 정규식을 취식할 수 없는 손님들을 위해 의학 및 영양학적인 전문지식을 바탕으로 구성된 식단이다. 고객의 요청 시 주문한 기내식에 대한 칼로리 정보의 제공이 된다. 이러한 식사 조절식에는 저지방식(Low fat meal), 당뇨식(Diabetic meal), 저열량식(Low calorie meal), 저단백식(Low protein meal), 고섬유소식(High fiber meal), 저염식(Low salt meal) 등이 있다.

셋째, 종교식에는 다음의 표와 같이 회교도식, 힌두교식 및 유대교식이 있다.

회교도식(Moslem)	힌두교식(Hindu)	유대교식(Kosher)
회교율법에 따라 준비된 음식으로 돼지고기 및 알코올을 사용하지 않음	힌두교도를 위한 특별식으로 쇠고기 및 돼지고기를 포함하지 않음	유대교 율법에 따라 고유의 전통 의식을 치른 후 만들어진 음식으로 완제품을 구매하여 제공됨

넷째, 영유아식의 경우 12개월 미만 영아에게는 액상분야와 아기용 주스가 제공되며, 12~24개월 미만 유아에게는 이유식과 아기용 주스가 제공된다. 아동식은 만 2세 이상~12세 미만의 어린이고객에게 제공되는 것으로 계절에 따라 카레라이스, 자장밥, 햄버거, 피자 등 아동들이 좋아하는 음식이 제공된다.

다섯째, 기타 특별식으로는 다음과 같이 해산물식, 과일식, 케이크 등이 있다.

해산물식	과일식	케이크
생선 및 해산물을 주 재료로 하여 곡류, 야채료, 과일류가 함께 제공됨	정규 기내식 대신 신선한 과일로만 구성되는 식사	생일과 허니문을 기념하기 위한 축하케이크(생일케이크 및 허니문 케이크)

기본 어휘

assorted	available	bar	base
brandy	Budweisers	choice	Cholesterol
cognac	coke	coupon	gin
heat	inconvenience	instead	juice
landing	loaded	manage	martini
meal	mistake	reservation	on board
portion	refill	reimburse	request
rocks(ice)	sample	scotch	seafood
set up	seven-up	shrimp	spill
tempura	tonic tray	turbulence	vegetarian
vodka	wipe		

1) Beverage service(음료 서비스)

Dialogue 1

음료 종류에 대한 문의

C: Cabin crew(Seward/Stewardess, P1: Passenger

C : Would you like something to drink?

P1 : What do you have?

C : We have juice, whiskey and beer.

P1 : What kind of juice do you have?

C : We have orange, apple, grapefruit and tomato juice.

P1 : Apple juice, please.

C : Here you are.

P1 : Thank you.

C : You're welcome.
(To the next passenger(P2)) How about you, sir?

Dialogue 2

음료 제공

C: Cabin crew(Seward/Stewardess, P: Passenger

C : Would you like something to drink?

P : Yes, I'll have an orange juice, please.

C : Certainly, sir. Here is your orange juice.
Enjoy your drink, sir.

Dialogue 3

다이어트 음료 요청

C: Cabin crew(Seward/Stewardess, P: Passenger

P : Excuse me. I'd like to have diet coke, please.

C : How about diet Pepsi?

P : That's O.K.

C : Here you go.

Dialogue 4

기내에서 제공되지 않는 음료 요청

C: Cabin crew(Seward/Stewardess, P: Passenger

C : Good evening, ma'am.
Would you care for something to drink?

P : Do you have any strawberry juice?

C : I'm sorry, but I'm afraid we don't have strawberry juice on board, ma'am.
We only have orange, pineapple and tomato juice.
What would you care for, ma'am?

P : I'll have tomato juice, then.

C : Sure, ma'am. Here is your tomato juice.
Enjoy your drink, ma'am.

Dialogue 5

추가 음료 요청

C: Cabin crew(Seward/Stewardess, P: Passenger

P : Excuse me, stewardess. Can I have another drink?

C : Sure, sir. What would you like?

P : Another martini, please.

C : ① Certainly, sir. Here you are.
May I take your glass, sir?
② Just a moment, please.
(......)

Here is your martini.

May I take your glass, sir?

Dialogue 6

음료 불평

C: Cabin crew(Seward/Stewardess, P: Passenger

P : Stewardess, my drink is too strong(weak).

C : I'm sorry, sir. I'll add some more tonic(more whisky, rum, gin, vodka, etc).

How is it now, sir?

P : Good.

C : I'm sorry for the inconvenience, sir.

Dialogue 7

음료잔 수거

C: Cabin crew(Seward/Stewardess, P: Passenger

C : Excuse me, sir.

Have you finished with your drink?

① P : Yes, I'm finished.

C : (taking glass ···) Thank you, sir.

② P : No, I'm not finished, yet.

C : Would you care for a refill?

2) Snack service(스낵 서비스)

Dialogue

C: Cabin crew(Seward/Stewardess, P: Passenger

C : Would you like to have a snack?

P : Yes, thank you.

3) Meal service(식사 서비스)

Dialogue 1 식사제공 1

C: Cabin crew(Seward/Stewardess, P: Passenger

C : Please return your seat to the upright position. We'll be serving meals, soon.
Would you pull out your table?

P : Sure.

C : We have beef and chicken.
Which one would you prefer?

P : Beef, please.

C : Would you like to drink some wine?
We have white wine and red wine.

P : Red wine, please.

C : Here you go. Enjoy your meal.

P : Thank you.

Dialogue 2

식사제공 2

C: Cabin crew(Seward/Stewardess, P1, P2: Passenger

C : We have a choice of New York steak and Chinese style shrimp. Which one would you prefer?

P1 : I'd like the shrimp, please.

C : Certainly, ma'am.
Would you mind opening your tray table, please?
Here is your shrimp.
(To the next passenger(P2)) How about you, sir?

P2 : I'll have the steak.

C : Certainly, sir. Here is your steak.
Enjoy your meal, sir.

Dialogue 3

식사제공 3(주요리가 다 떨어졌을 경우)

C: Cabin crew(Seward/Stewardess, P: Passenger

C : Here is your meal, ma'am

P : Excuse me. What kind of meal is this?

C : It's Chinese style shrimp, ma'am.

P : I don't like shrimp very much. The menu says you have a choice of shrimp and steak.
Don't you have any steak?

C : I'm sorry, ma'am, but I'm afraid we've run out of the steak.

P : I see.

C : I'm sorry, ma'am. I hope you enjoy your meal.

Dialogue 4

커피 서비스 1

C: Cabin crew(Seward/Stewardess, P: Passenger

C : Would you like some coffee, sir?

P : Yes, please.

C : May I have your cup, please? Thank you, sir.
Here is your coffee, sir.

P : I'll need some cream and sugar.

C : They are on your tray, sir.

Dialogue 5

커피 서비스 2

C: Cabin crew(Seward/Stewardess, P: Passenger

C: Would you care for some more coffee, sir?

① P: Yes, please.

C: May I have your cup, please?
Thank you. Here you are, sir.

② P: No, thanks. I've had enough.

Dialogue 6

홍차 서비스

C: Cabin crew(Seward/Stewardess, P: Passenger

C1 : Would you like some tea, sir?

P : Yes, I'd like some tea, please.

C1 : Certainly, sir.
Another attendant will serve tea shortly.
(……)

C2 : Would you care for some tea, sir?

P : Yes, please.

C2 : May I have your cup, please? Thank you, sir.
Would you care for some lemon?

P : Yes, please.

C2 : Certainly, sir. Here is your tea. Enjoy your drink, sir.

Dialogue 7

식사를 마친 후 1

C: Cabin crew(Seward/Stewardess, P: Passenger

C : May I take your meal tray, sir?

P : Yes, please.

C : I hope you enjoyed your meal.

P : It was delicious.

C : I'm glad to hear that.

Dialogue 8

식사를 마친 후 2

C: Cabin crew(Seward/Stewardess, P: Passenger

C : May I take your meal tray, sir?

P : No, I'm not finished, yet.

C : I'm sorry, sir.
Please take your time and enjoy your meal.

Dialogue 9

특별주문 1

C: Cabin crew(Seward/Stewardess, P: Passenger

P : Excuse me, stewardess. When I made my reservation, I requested a low cholesterol meal.

C : I'm sorry, sir. May I have your name, please?

P : My name is Steven Chigal.

C : Thank you, sir.

I'll check on your meal immediately, sir.

(……)

Thank you for waiting, sir. We are preparing your meal now. It'll be ready soon.

(……)

Here is your meal, sir. I'm sorry for the inconvenience. Enjoy your meal.

Dialogue 10

특별주문 2

C: Cabin crew(Seward/Stewardess, P: Passenger

P : Excuse me, stewardess. I requested a vegetarian meal when I made a reservation.

C : I'm sorry, sir. May I have your name, please?

P : Yes. I'm Charles Kim.

C : Thank you, sir. I'll check on your meal immediately.

(……)

I'm very sorry, sir, but your meal wasn't loaded in Seoul. Our ground staff made a mistake. Please accept our apologies. Instead, would you care for a vegetable salad, sir? Perhaps a plate of assorted fruit, cheese and vegetables, sir?

P : Well, alright.

C : Just a moment, please.

(······)

Here is your salad, sir.

I hope you enjoy your meal.

Useful Expressions

- Would you care for *something to drink* before dinner?
  some more wine
  something else

- We have *scotch, juice, soft drinks and beer.*
  orange, apple and tomato juice
  beef and chicken

- Which *would you like?*
  do you prefer
  one would you care for

- How would you like your vodka, sir?

- Here is your ___________, sir.

- I'm sorry, ma'am, but I'm afraid we only *have chicken available.*
  offer scotch and beer on this portion

- All we have *are orange, apple and tomato juice,* ma'am.
  is Johnnie Walker scotch

- *Have you finished with your drink,* sir?
  May I take your glass

- Would you *care for a refill?*
  like another one

- May I *take your glass,* please?
  clear your table
  take your cup
  have your meal tray

- Excuse me, ma'am.
  Would you mind opening your table, please?

- Another cabin attendant will serve tea and coffee shortly.

- Some more *cream & sugar?*
  wine
  coffee

- How about you, sir?

- I hope you enjoy(ed) your meal, sir.

3. In-flight entertainment(기내 오락서비스)

기내 식사 전·후 손님들은 기내에서 제공되는 각종 오락서비스를 받게 된다. 이러한 서비스에는 최신영화, 다큐멘터리, 스포츠, 드라마, 세계음악, 최신가요, 게임 등 항공사가 엄선한 오락 프로그램이 있으며, 손님들은 기내 메인화면이나 좌석에 장착된 개인용 모니터를 통해 채널별로 제공되는 영화, 단편물, 음악, 운항정보, 기내면세품 안내 등 다양한 콘텐츠를 즐길 수 있다. 국제선과 같이 장시간 비행의 경우 손님들은 식사 후 제공된 이어폰을 이용해 기내 영화를 한두 편 정도 감상하게 된다. 대부분의 항공사는 기내 음악으로 현대음악과 고전음악을 구비하고 있다. 손님들은 좌석의 양쪽에 있는 채널을 이용하여 음악을 선택해서 들을 수 있으며, 영화프로그램은 좌석 앞주머니에 있는 기내책자를 참조하여 선택하여 즐길 수 있다.

영화감상 전에 기내 승무원들은 모든 손님들이 영화를 볼 준비가 되어 있는지를 둘러보아야 한다. 모든 창문 가리개는 닫혀져야 하며, 스크린 앞의 좌석에 앉은 손님들은 영화를 보다 잘 볼 수 있는 위치로 이동해야 하며, 책을 읽고 싶은 손님들을 위해서는 독서등이 켜져야 한다. 모든 준비가 완료된 후에 손님은 약 1시간 30분 정도의 영화를 기내에서 즐기게 된다. 영화가 시작되면 승무원들은 이어폰 사용법을 잘 모르는 손님들을 도와주도록 노력한다.

이 시간은 승무원들이 휴식을 취하는 시간으로 손님 호출에 대비한 최소한의 인원을 제외하고는 기내 승무원 침실(cabin bunk)에서 교대로 휴식을 취하게 된다.

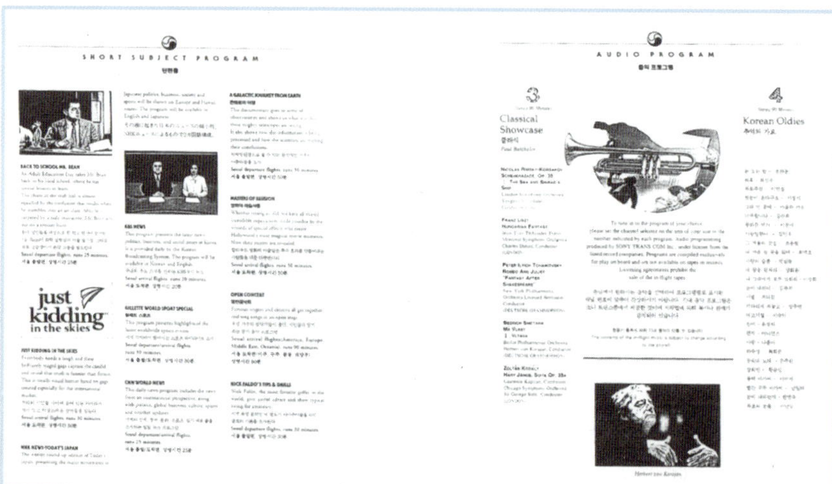

기본 어휘

bulkhead	channel selector	charge	classical
earphone jack	jazz	music program	out of order
pamphlet	pop	rock	seat pocket
show	sound system	volume control	

1) Information request(손님 문의)

Dialogue 1

기내 음악 문의

C: Cabin crew(Seward/Stewardess, P: Passenger

P : What kind of music do you have?

C : (taking out in-flight music pamphlet from seat pocket)
We have rock, jazz, pop and classical music.
This pamphlet will show you today's in-flight music program, sir.

Dialogue 2

영화정보 문의

C: Cabin crew(Seward/Stewardess, P: Passenger

P : When are you showing the movie today?

C : The movie will be shown right after the meal, sir.

P : When are you going to show a movie?

C : It will start in 10 minutes.

P : What's the title of the movie?

C : It will be 'Forest Gump' starring Tom Hanks.

P : Can I get some earphones for the movie?

C : Yes, but there is a 3 dollar charge for a headset.

P : Here's 3 dollars. What channel is the movie on?

C : Channel 2.

2) Earphone set problems(이어폰 불량)

Dialogue 1

불량 이어폰 수리

C: Cabin crew(Seward/Stewardess, P: Passenger

P : Excuse me. I don't think my earphones are working.

C : Let me check them, sir.

(after checking volume control, channel selector, and whether earphone jack is firmly in place)

Can you hear anything now?

P : Now they're working. Thank you.

C : You're welcome.

Dialogue 2

불량 이어폰으로 인한 손님 좌석 이동

C: Cabin crew(Seward/Stewardess, P: Passenger

P : Excuse me, miss. This earphone set is out of order.

C : Excuse me, sir. Can you hear through them now?

P : No, still nothing at all.

C : I don't know what's wrong. Just a moment, please.

(Stewardess gets a new set of earphones and checks a nearby empty seat's music system.)

Would you like to move to this seat over here, sir? The sound system in this seat is working better.

Dialogue 3 불량 이어폰 수리불능 및 손님 좌석 이동 불능

C: Cabin crew(Seward/Stewardess, P: Passenger

P : Excuse me. This earphone doesn't work.

C : Excuse me, sir. Can you hear it now, sir?

P : No, still nothing at all.

C : I'm sorry, but I'm afraid all the seats are occupied, sir.

P : Oh, don't worry. It's OK.

C : I'm sorry, sir. Would you care for a newspaper or something to drink?

P : No, that's alright.

3) Bulkhead passenger at movie time(스크린 앞쪽 손님)

Dialogue 1 좌석 여분이 있을 때

C: Cabin crew(Seward/Stewardess, P: Passenger

C : Excuse me, ma'am.
Are you going to watch the movie?

P : Yes, I am.

C : I'm afraid you won't be able to see the screen very well from this seat. Would you like to change seats? We have some empty seats in the middle of the cabin.

P : Yes, I guess I'd better.

C : This way, please.
(......)
Here is your seat, ma'am. I hope you enjoy the movie.

Dialogue 2

좌석 여분이 없을 때

C: Cabin crew(Seward/Stewardess, P: Passenger

P : Excuse me, stewardess. I can't see the movie screen from this seat. Are there any empty seats in the middle of the cabin?

C : I'm sorry, but I'm afraid all the other seats are occupied, sir. I'm sorry for the inconvenience, sir.

movie program 영화 프로그램 안내

for First Class Business & Economy Class

profiteers. Assigned to assist Kelly locate and recover the stolen weapons is Col. Thomas Devoe (George Clooney), an unorthodox military intelligence officer.

백악관 핵무기 단속반의 책임자이자 핵물리학자인 줄리아 켈리 박사(니콜 키드먼 扮)는 핵폭발 사고가 핵무기의 유출을 덮어버리기 위한 러시아 테러리스트들의 음모임을 알게 된다. 육군 특수 정보국 토마스 드보 대령(조지 클루니 扮)은 도난당한 핵무기를 다시 찾기 위한 계획에 켈리의 보좌역으로 참여하게 되는데…….

PICTURE PERFECT
픽처 퍼펙트

Genre: Comedy / Starring: Jennifer Aniston, Kevin Bacon / Director: Glenn Gordon Caron / Running Time: 100 minutes / Rated: PG-13

Jennifer Aniston, of the phenomenally successful TV series *Friends*, stars in this romantic comedy about a single woman who, to jump-start a promising career in advertising, uses a random photo to invent a fictional fiance. When her boss asks to meet the new man in her life, she asks the guy in the picture to help her with her predicament—and he's only too happy to oblige. Her world is subsequently turned upside-down as romantic complications follow. From the creator of *Moonlighting*.

인기 TV 시리즈 '프렌즈'에 출연했던 제니퍼 애니스톤이 광고 분야에서 일하는 독신 여성으로 나온다. 그녀는 더 나은 직위를 얻기 위해 거짓말로 무심코 집은 사진 속의 남자를 약혼자라고 말한다. 어느날 상관이 남자 친구가 있는지를 묻자 다급해진 그녀는 그에게 약혼자 역할을 부탁하고, 그는 기꺼이 그 제안을 받아들인다. 이후 그들 사이에는 미묘한 감정의 흐름이 생겨나는데…….

GEORGE OF THE JUNGLE
조지 오브 더 정글

Genre: Comedy / Starring: Brendan Fraser, Leslie Mann, Thomas Haden Church / Director: Sam Weisman / Running Time: 92 minutes / Rated: PG

One of TV's most beloved cartoon heroes, George makes his debut on the silver screen in this irresistible comedy-action adventure. Living in the jungle with his animal pals—the wise ape, the Tookie Tookie bird, the trusty elephant Shep—George (Brendan Fraser) has an idyllic (if accident-prone) life. When he meets the beautiful career woman Ursula (Leslie Mann), he finds the opportunity to live as a human with all the comforts of modern-day life, and must decide where he really belongs.

TV에서 가장 사랑받았던 만화 주인공 중 한 명인 조지. 그가 이 코미디 액션 어드벤처로 영화에 데뷔한다. 정글에서 원숭이, 코끼리 등의 동물 친구들과 함께 살고 있는 조지(브렌던 프레이저 扮)는 목가적인 삶을 영위하고 있다. 그는 우연히 아름다운 캐리어 우먼 우슬라(레슬리 만 扮)를 만나게 되고, 안락하고 현대적인 삶을 함께 나눌 수 있는 기회를 얻게 된다.

ROCKET MAN
로켓 맨

Genre: Comedy / Starring: Harland Williams, Jessica Lundy, William Sadler, Jeffrey DeMunn / Director: Stuart Gillard / Running Time: 94 minutes / Rated: PG

When a member of the first manned mission to Mars is injured during training, NASA reluctantly accepts the only possible candidate for his replacement, Fred Randall (Harland Williams), who, for a rocket scientist, is no rocket scientist. The inept Fred disrupts the crew, butts heads with the cocky captain, and falls hopelessly in love with a beautiful officer. With his best pal, a trained chimpanzee named Ulysses, Fred manages to create constant comic chaos on the voyage to the Red Planet.

화성에 파견할 사람들 중 하나가 훈련 도중 부상하자, NASA는 어쩔 수 없이 그를 대신할 사람을 뽑는다. 하지만 로켓 연구자로 임명된 프레드 랜덜(할랜드 윌리엄스 扮)은 이와는 전혀 상관이 없는 인물. 우여곡절 끝에 훈련에 합류한 프레드와 그의 절친한 동료인 침팬지 율리시즈는 승무원들을 혼란에 빠뜨리고, 잘난 척하는 상관과 충돌하고, 장교와 사랑에 빠지는 등 좌충우돌하며 화성까지의 항해를 혼란 상태로 만들어 버린다.

4) Preparation for showing movies(영화상영 준비)

Dialogue 1 창문 내림

C: Cabin crew(Seward/Stewardess, P: Passenger

C : Excuse me, sir. Would you mind closing your window shade, please? We will be showing the movie shortly.

P : No, of course not.

C : Thank you, sir. I hope you enjoy the movie.

Dialogue 2 독서등 사용

C: Cabin crew(Seward/Stewardess, P: Passenger

C : Excuse me, ma'am. We'll be showing the movie soon. Would you mind if I close the shade, please?

P : I'm not going to watch the movie.
I'm going to read, instead.

C : Certainly, ma'am. But I'm afraid we have to close the window shades while the movie is showing. Would you like me to turn on the reading light, ma'am?
(……)
Thank you. Would you care for something to drink?

P : No, thank you.

C : Enjoy the flight, ma'am.

Useful Expressions

- This pamphlet will show you today's in-flight music program, sir.
- Here's a pamphlet on today's movie, ma'am.
- The movie will be shown right after *the meal*, sir.

  dinner
- I hope you enjoy the movie, ma'am.
- Today's *presentation* is "Terminator II."

  movie
- I'm afraid you won't be able to see the screen very well from this seat, sir.
  Would you like to change seats?
- Would you mind if I close the window shade?
  We'll be showing the movie soon.
- We have to close the shade while the movie is showing.
- Would you like me to turn on the reading light, sir?

NOTES:

4. Service and comfort(서비스와 편의제공)

비행기를 처음 타는 손님이나 몇 번 타보지 못한 손님들은 호출등 소등버튼(call reset button), 음량 조절기(volume control), 채널 선택 다이얼(channel selector dials), 이어폰 작동방법이나 의자를 뒤로 젖히고 앞으로 당기는 방법 등과 같은 기내 시설물들의 사용방법을 알지 못할 때 당황하게 된다. 또한 손님들은 장시간의 비행으로 인해 지루함을 느낄 수 있고, 수면을 취하지 못하는 손님들은 괴로움을 느끼기까지 한다.

이럴 때 승무원은 위 시설물들의 사용방법을 손님에게 친절히 알려줌으로써 손님으로 하여금 편안한 휴식을 취하게 하고, 손님에게 담요와 베개를 제공하여 수면을 원하는 손님에게 도움을 줄 수 있어야 한다. 또한 승무원은 손님들에게 신문이나 잡지를 제공하여 지루함을 덜어주고, 맥주와 같은 간단한 주류를 제공하여 불면증에 시달리는 손님을 도와줘야 한다.

기본 어휘

adjust	blanket	channel	forward
knob	lean back(forward)	pillow	plug in
recline	upright position	ventilation	volume control

Dialogue 1

서비스시설 사용법을 모르는 손님

C: Cabin crew(Seward/Stewardess, P: Passenger

P : Excuse me. How do I adjust the ventilation?

C : Please turn the knob, sir.

P : And how do I adjust the volume?

C : Just turn this dial, sir.
Do you know how to change channels?

P : I have no idea.

C : Just turn this dial, sir.

P : Will you show me how I turn on and off the light?

C : Please push the switch that looks like a light bulb.

P : Where can I plug in the earphone?

C : Right here, sir.

P : I'm very sorry, but I have one more question. How do I recline my seat and return it to the upright position?

C : Just push this button, lean back and lean forward.

P : Thank you very much.

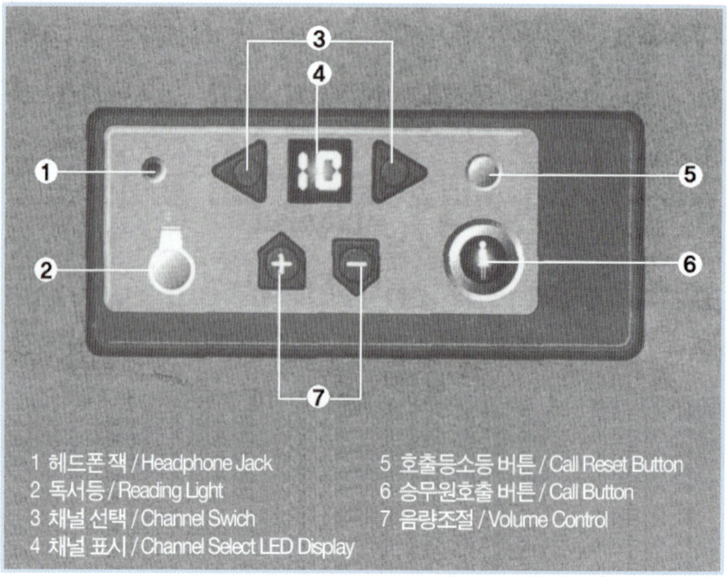

Dialogue 2

춥거나 불편해 보이는 손님

C: Cabin crew(Seward/Stewardess, P: Passenger

C: Would you like a blanket, ma'am?

P: Yes, please.

C: (covering the passenger) And here's a pillow.
Would you care for some hot tea or coffee, ma'am?

① P: No, thank you.

C: Well, let us know if you need anything else.

② P: Yes, please.

(……)

C : Here is your tea/coffee, ma'am. Have a nice rest.

(After a few minutes later)

C : Excuse me, ma'am. Are you feeling alright? Would you like to lie down? We have an empty row in the back. Would that be alright?

P : Oh, yes. Thank you.

C : You're welcome. This way, please.

(……)

Here is your seat.

Would you like a pillow and blanket, ma'am?

P : Yes, please.

C : I hope you feel better.

Dialogue 3

지루한 고객

C: Cabin crew(Seward/Stewardess, P: Passenger

C : (With a smile) Are you enjoying the flight, sir?

P : I guess so.

C : Would you care for some coffee?

P : Yes, please. How long will it be before we get to Washington, D.C.?

C : We expect to arrive in about three hours.

P : I see.

C : Would you care for a newspaper or magazine?

P : Do you have 'The Times'?

C : Certainly, sir. Just a moment, please.

(……)

Here is the magazine you requested, sir.

Dialogue 4

신혼부부의 사진촬영 요청

C: Cabin crew(Seward/Stewardess, P: Passenger

P : Excuse me. Would you mind taking our picture? We're on our honeymoon.

C : Oh, really? Congratulations!
I'd be glad to take your picture.

P : Just push the button, please.

C : All right. Are you ready? Cheese! There you go.

P : Thank you very much.

C : You're welcome.
I hope you have a wonderful honeymoon.

Dialogue 5

시끄럽게 떠드는 어린이 손님

C: Cabin crew(Seward/Stewardess, P1, P2: Passenger

P1 : Excuse me, stewardess. I'm trying to get some rest, but that little boy is making so much noise. Can't you do something about it?

C : I'm sorry for the inconvenience.
Just a moment, please.
(to a little boy)

C : Hi! What's your name?

P2 : Tim.

C : How old are you?

P2 : Four.

C : Do you want some orange juice?

P2 : Yes.

C : I see. You are a good boy. Where is your seat, Tim?

Dialogue 6

잠에서 깨어나는 손님

C: Cabin crew(Seward/Stewardess, P: Passenger

C : Good morning, sir. Did you have a good sleep?
Would you care for some orange juice?

P : Oh, yeah. Please.

C : Certainly, sir.
(······)
Here is your orange juice.
We'll be serving breakfast shortly.

Dialogue 7

손님과의 대화

C: Cabin crew(Seward/Stewardess, P: Passenger

C : Good morning. Are you enjoying the flight?

P : Yes, it's been great.

C : Is this your first visit to Korea?

P : No, I visited Korea during the '88 Seoul Olympics.

C : I see. I hope you enjoy your stay in Korea.

Useful Expressions

- Would you like a *blanket?*
  pillow
- Would you care for some coffee, ma'am?
- Did you *sleep well?*
  have a good sleep
  have a nice rest
- Let us know if you need anything else.
- Are you feeling alright?
- I hope you enjoy your stay in Korea.

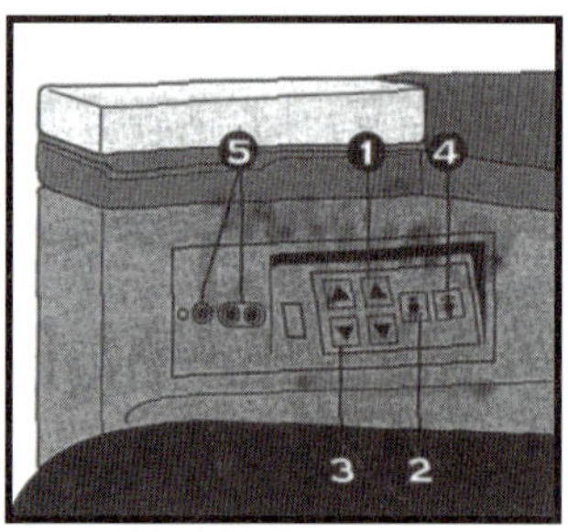

FIRST, PRESTIGE & ECONOMY CLASS (B747-400, MD 11)

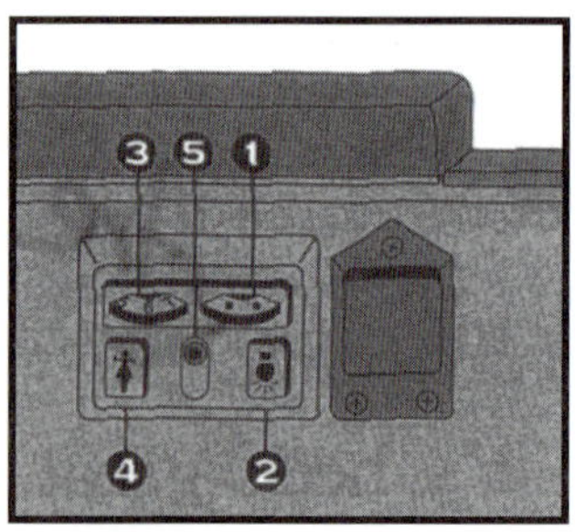

FIRST, PRESTIGE & ECONOMY CLASS (B747-300)

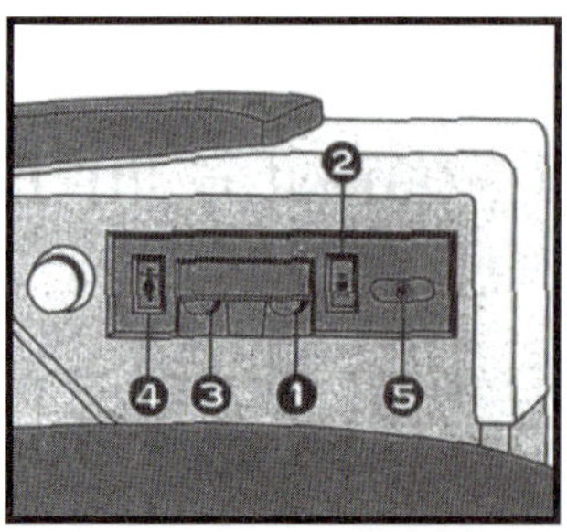

FIRST & PRESTIGE CLASS(B747-200)

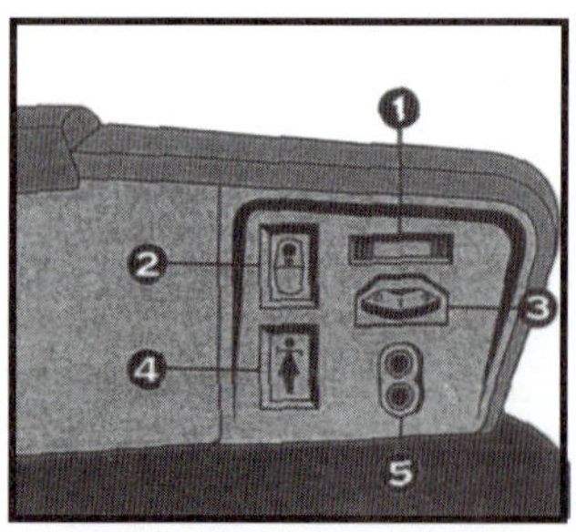

ECONOMY CLASS(B747-200)

5. Sick passenger handling(환자 서비스)

손님의 입장에서 비행 중에 가장 괴로운 순간 중의 하나는 아마도 비행기 멀미일 것이다. 집을 떠나서 누구도 이국에서 자신을 돌봐주는 사람이 없을 때 손님들은 철저하게 무기력함을 느끼게 된다. 그래서 손님의 입장에서 여행 중에 건강을 유지하는 것이 정말로 중요하게 된다.

기내에는 멀미약, 감기약, 소화제 등과 같은 비상약들이 구비되어 있다. 또한 기내 승무원들은 손님들이 아플 때 어떠한 조치를 취해야 하는가를 잘 숙지하고 있다.

빈번하게 일어나지는 않지만, 어떤 경우에는 비행 중에 심각한 증세가 발생하면 비행기는 근처 공항이나 혹은 출발지 공항으로 되돌아가기도 한다. 만일 기내에 의사나 간호사가 타고 있다면 비상치료를 위해 이들의 요청을 구할 수 있으며, 환자가 병원에 옮겨지기까지 가능한 모든 조치를 취해야 한다. 모든 승무원들은 환자 손님에 대해 진심 어린 관심과 동정적인 태도를 보여줘야 하며, 각종 병명 및 관련된 표현들을 잘 숙지하고 있어야 한다.

기본 어휘

airsick	allorgy	aspirin	antacid
blocked nose	chilly/chills	cold	diarrhea
dizzy	earache	fever	flue
hangover	headache	indigestion	migraine
nausea	nose bleed	rash	runny nose
sore throat	stuffy nose	temperature	throw up
toothache	upset stomach	vomit	

Dialogue 1

두통 손님

C: Cabin crew(Seward/Stewardess, P: Passenger

P : I don't feel well.

C : What's the matter?

P : I think I have a headache.

Do you have any medicine?

C : Please wait a minute.

(……)

Here is some aspirin. You should take two tablets.

P : Thank you.

C : How are you feeling?

P : A lot better, thank you.

Dialogue 2

감기 손님

C: Cabin crew(Seward/Stewardess, P: Passenger

C : You look pale. Are you O.K.?

P : No, I don't think so. I've got a bad cold, and my nose is blocked. Do you have any aspirin?

C : I'm sorry, sir, but I'm afraid we don't have aspirin on board. Would you care for hot tea with lemon?

P : Yes, please.

C : Certainly, sir. Just a moment, please.

(……)

Here is your tea, sir. I hope you'll feel better.

Dialogue 3

멀미 손님 1

C: Cabin crew(Seward/Stewardess, P: Passenger

P : Excuse me. I think I might get sick.

Can I have some medicine, please?

C : Oh! I'm sorry to hear that. We have some anti—airsickness medicine.

Will that be alright?

P : Thank you very much.

C : I hope you feel better.

If you need anything else, please let us know.

Dialogue 4 멀미 손님 2

C: Cabin crew(Seward/Stewardess, P: Passenger

P : Excuse me, I feel like vomiting(throwing up).

C : Here is an airsick bag for you just in case you vomit, sir. Is there anything I can do for you, sir?

P : Yes, do you have any medicine?

C : Yes, sir. But I'm afraid it is for cabin crew use only. It is called Bonaling-A, which is Korean brand equivalent to the Drammamine. Would that be alright?

P : Yes, I'll have that.

C : Certainly, sir. Just a moment, please.

(……)

Here is your tablet, sir.

P : Thank you very much.

C : You're welcome. I hope you feel better.

(A few minutes later)

How are you feeling, sir? Can I get you anything else?

Useful Expressions

- I hope you feel better.
- How are you feeling now, sir?
  Can I get you anything(else)?
- I'm sorry, but we don't have anything for a sore throat.
- It is a Korean brand equivalent to the Aspirin / Drammamine.

NOTES:

6. In-flight sales(기내 면세품 판매)

기내 승무원의 중요한 임무 중 하나는 손님들에게 면세품을 판매하는 것이다. 많은 손님들은 사전예약주문제도(손님이 해외여행을 하기 전에 원하는 면세품을 미리 주문하고, 해당편 항공기 기내에서 주문품을 전달받는 방법)나 기내 판매를 통해 지인들에게 선물 또는 기념품을 사게 된다. 특히 스케줄이 꽉 짜인 비즈니스 클래스 손님에게는 기내 판매가 중요한 판매기회가 된다.

손님들은 기내 면세품 구입시 별도의 한도액은 없으나 입국하는 국가의 면세허용 범위를 준수해야 한다. 면세품의 종류는 술, 담배로부터 화장품, 실크 넥타이, 금도금 펜 등 다양하다. 승무원들은 모든 종류의 외국통화와 환율을 숙지하여야 하며, 손님들로부터의 팁은 사양해야 한다.

기본 어휘

allowance	apron	Ballantine 17	Camus Napoleon
carton	Chanel No. 5	Chivas Regal	Christian Dior
conversion rate	cosmetic	countersign	Courvoisier Napoleon
currency	Dunhill Old	Elizabeth Arden	duty-free items
Hennessy X.O.	Hermes	scarf	Johnnie Walker
Lancome	Martel X.O.	Master	Nina Ricci
Mild Seven	Parliament	refund	Royal Salute
souvenir	Swatch watch	ties	traveller's check
Yves Saint Laurent			

1) Information request(손님 문의)

Dialogue 1 면세품 허용정보 문의

C: Cabin crew(Seward/Stewardess, P: Passenger

P : Do you know how much perfume I can take into Hong Kong?

C : This pamphlet will show you the perfume allowance for Hong Kong, sir. You may take in 60ml of perfume.

P : Oh, I see. Thank you.
C : You're welcome, sir.

Dialogue 2

면세품 종류 문의

C: Cabin crew(Seward/Stewardess, P: Passenger

C : Excuse me. Would you like to buy any duty-free items, ma'am?
P : Yes, what kinds of cigarettes do you sell?
C : We have Mild Seven, Kent, Marlboro and Korean cigarettes.

Dialogue 3

면세품 주문

C: Cabin crew(Seward/Stewardess, P: Passenger

C : May I take your order for any duty-free items, sir?
P : Yes, what do you have?
C : We have alcohol, souvenirs, cosmetics, cigarettes and perfumes for sale, sir. This shopping guide will tell you about our in-flight sales, sir.

2) Duty-free item sales(면세품 판매)

Dialogue 1

판매 1

C: Cabin crew(Seward/Stewardess, P: Passenger

P : How much is Gucci perfume?
C : Twenty dollars, ma'am.
P : Can I pay in Korean won?

C : Sure, you can.
P : How much is it in won?
C : Thirty thousand won, please.

Dialogue 2

거스름 돈이 있는 경우 1

C: Cabin crew(Seward/Stewardess, P: Passenger

C : Would you like any duty-free items?
P : I would like to buy scotch.
Do you have Chivas Regal?
C : Yes, we do. How many bottles would you like?
P : One, please. How much is it?
C : Twenty-five dollars, sir.
P : Here's 30 dollars.
C : Here's your change.
P : Thank you.

Dialogue 3

거스름 돈이 있는 경우 2

C: Cabin crew(Seward/Stewardess, P: Passenger

C : Excuse me, would you like to buy any duty-free items, sir?
P : Could I have two cartons of Marlboro and a bottle of Chivas Regal?
C : Certainly sir. Here you are. That will be $ 40, please.
P : Here's 50 dollars.
C : Thank you, sir. Here is your change, 10 dollars.

Dialogue 4 거스름 돈이 없는 경우

C: Cabin crew(Seward/Stewardess, P: Passenger

P : I'm sorry, but all I have is a 100 dollar bill.
Do you have change?

C : Oh, I'm sorry. I'm afraid I don't have change right now, sir. I will bring your change as soon as possible. Would that be alright?
(Write down seat number, the amount received, cost of item and name.)
......
I am sorry to have kept you waiting, sir.
Here is your change, $ 60. Is that correct, sir?

P : Thank you.

C : You're welcome, sir.

Dialogue 5 신용카드 사용시

C: Cabin crew(Seward/Stewardess, P: Passenger

P : Excuse me. Do you accept traveller's checks?

① C : Yes, sir.

P : Here you are.

② C : No, I am sorry. We only accept U.S. dollars(won, yen).

Dialogue 6 환 불

C: Cabin crew(Seward/Stewardess, P: Passenger

P : Excuse me. Would I be able to get a refund on these cosmetics?

C : Could you tell me where you bought them, sir?

P : I bought them at the airport duty-free shop.

C : I'm sorry, but I'm afraid we can only give refunds on items purchased during the flight, sir.

P : I see. Thank you.

DUTY FREE

주류 **Liquors**

1 조니 워커 골드(1*l*)
Johnnie Walker Gold Label (1*l*) — ***$65***

2 미들톤(아이리쉬 위스키, 700ml)
Midleton(Irish whiskey, 700ml) — ***$120***

3 글렌피딕(18년, 700ml)
Glenfiddich(18 Years Old, 700ml) — ***$80***

4 조니 워커 블루(750ml)
Johnnie Walker Blue Label (750ml) — ***$120***

5 올드 파(12년, 1*l*)
Old Parr(12 Years Old, 1 *l*) — ***$28***

6 발렌타인(17년, 750ml)
Ballantine's(17 Years Old, 750ml) — ***$49***

7 로열 살루트(21년, 700ml)
Royal Salute(21 Years Old, 700ml) — ***$85***

8 시바스 리갈(12년, 1 *l*)
Chivas Regal(12 Years Old, 1 *l*) — ***$28***

9 발렌타인(30년, 750ml)
Ballantine's(30 Years Old, 750ml) — ***$235***

가격 및 기타 사항은 기내 Seat pocket에 있는 SKY SHOP을 참조하여 주시기 바랍니다.
For further information about duty free in-flight shopping, please refer to the SKY SHOP catalogue in your seat pocket.

DUTY FREE

특선품 Selected Items

1 미키모토 진주 귀걸이(A) (18金, 안 뚫은 귀용)
Mikimoto Pearl Earrings
(W/18K Gold, Screw Type) — ***$240***

2 미키모토 진주 목걸이(B) (18金)
Mikimoto Pearl Pendant(W/18K Gold) — ***$240***

3 미키모토 진주 목걸이(C) (18金)
Mikimoto Pearl Pendant
(W/18K Gold) — ***$240***

4 미키모토 진주 목걸이(D) (18金)
Mikimoto Pearl Pendant
(W/18K Gold) — ***$240***

5 모네 액세서리 세트(23K 3중 도금)
Monet Accessory Set
(23K Triple Gold Plated) — ***$64***

NEW

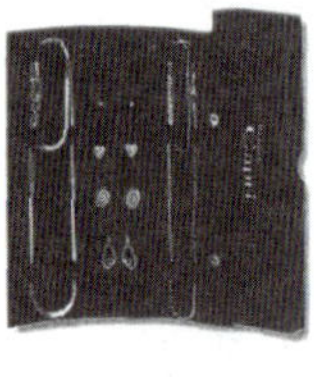

6 비쥬 카프리 쥬얼리 세트(뚫은 귀용 귀걸이 4쌍, 목걸이 2개, 팔찌2개)(18K 4중 도금)
Bijoux Capri Jewelry Set
(Pin Type Earring 4pairs, Necklace 2pieces, Bracelet 2pieces) (18K Quadruple Gold Plated) — ***$48***

7 자수정 목걸이, 귀걸이(뚫은 귀용) 세트 (24K 3중 도금/총 5.5캐럿)
Amethyst Pendant, Earring (Pin Type) **Set**
(24K Triple Gold Plated/ Total 5.5 Carat) — ***$67***

8 자수정 목걸이 (5.5캐럿)
Amethyst Pendant(5.5 Carat) — ***$60***

가격 및 기타 사항은 기내 Seat pocket에 있는 SKY SHOP을 참조하여 주시기 바랍니다.
For further information about duty free in-flight shopping, please refer to the SKY SHOP catalogue in your seat pocket.

DUTY FREE

화장품 Cosmetics

1 에스떼 로데 콤플리트 피니시(콤팩트) (19g)
Estée Lauder Complete Finish(19g) — *$21*

2 게르랭 브러시
Guerlain Brush — *$62*

3 랑꼼 세뒥써옹 쿨뛰르 메이크업
Lancôme Séduction Couleur Make-up — *$40*

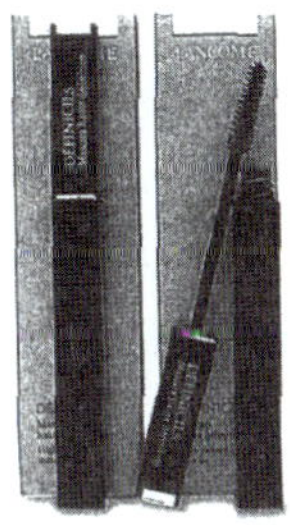

4 랑꼼 데피니씰 마스카라 듀오 세트(2개)
Lancôme Definicils Mascara Duo Set(2pieces) — ***$40***

5 에스떼 로데 립스틱 세트(3색/3개)
Estée Lauder Lipstick Set (3colors/3pieces) — ***$35***

6 쉬 드 파리 립스틱 세트(6개)
Chic de Paris Lipstick Set (6pieces) — ***$33***

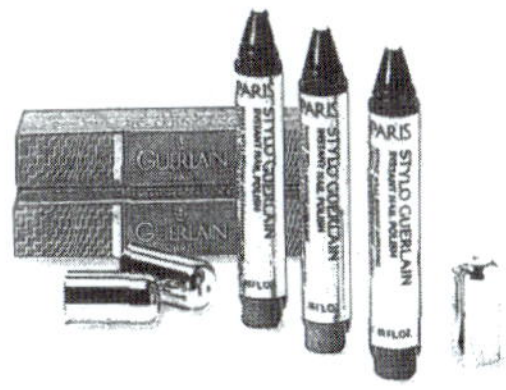

7 게르랭 인스턴트 네일 폴리시 트리오(15.9ml)
Guerlain Instant Nail Polish Trio (15.9ml) — ***$53***

가격 및 기타 사항은 기내 Seat pocket에 있는 SKY SHOP을 참조하여 주시기 바랍니다.
For further information about duty free in-flight shopping, please refer to the SKY SHOP catalogue in your seat pocket.

Useful Expressions

- This pamphlet will show you the duty-free allowance for ______________.
- You may take in ________ of perfume and ________ of whiskey.
- Excuse me, would you like to buy any duty-free items, ma'am?
- May I have your order for any duty-free items, sir?
- What would you like, sir?
- *Would you like to buy any duty-free items*, ma'am?
  What would you like
  May I help you
- We have *Kent, Marlboro, Mild Seven and Korean cigarettes.*
  Johnnie Walker, and Chivas Regal
  Chanel No. 5, Nina Ricci, Christian Dior
  Johnnie Walker Black, Ballantine 17, Camus
- I'm sorry, but I'm afraid it has sold out, ma'am.
  Would you care for ______, instead?
- *It will be* $ ________, please.
  That will be
  It comes to
- We accept *traveler's checks.*
  Visa card
- I'm sorry, but we do not accept that currency.
  Do you have any other currency, sir?
- Please countersign it and print your name and passport number on the back, sir.

- I'm sorry but I'm afraid I don't have change right now, sir. I will bring your change as soon as I can. Would that be alright, sir?
- Here is your change, $_______. Is that correct, sir?
- May I ask where you bought it, ma'am?
- Could you kindly tell me where you made the purchase?
- Where did you buy ________, ma'am?
- I'm sorry, but I'm afraid we can only give refunds on items purchased during the flight, sir.
- Thank you. Here is your refund.

NOTES:

7. CIQ Information(세관, 입국 및 검역 안내)

비행기가 목적지에 가까워오면 승무원들은 다시 한번 목적지에 대한 손님들의 질문으로 바빠지게 된다. 질문들은 대개 CIQ(Customs, Immigration and Quarantine) 절차와 도시 정보에 관한 것들이다. 많은 손님들이 짧은 시간에 공항터미널에 도착하기 때문에 손님들은 CIQ 신고서를 작성할 시간과 장소를 갖지 못하게 된다. 그래서 승무원들은 목적지 도착 전에 CIQ 직원들을 위해 손님들이 작성할 신고서들을 손님들에게 나눠준다. 승무원들은 목적지를 처음 가는 손님들을 위해 도움을 주어야 한다. 특히 이민수속과 세관검사가 엄격한 몇몇 나라에 가서는 돈을 일정액 이상 소지하거나 비싼 물건을 가지고 가는 손님들은 반드시 세관신고카드에 신고해야 한다. 참고로 통과손님들은 CIQ 절차를 거치지 않아도 된다.

alien	board	citizen	confirm
CIQ(Customs, Immigration, Quarantine)			customs
declare	declaration	disembarkation	embarkation
fill out	form	migrant	on business
passport number	pleasure	reservation	resident
tourist	transit	valuables	visitor

Dialogue 1

거주자의 경우

C: Cabin crew(Seward/Stewardess, P: Passenger

P : Excuse me. When I left Korea, they put this ED card(=embarkation card) in my passport.
Do I have to fill it out again?

C : Are you a resident?

P : Yes, I am.

C : Please just fill in our flight number, and the place of departure.

Dialogue 2

여행객의 경우

C: Cabin crew(Seward/Stewardess, P: Passenger

P : Excuse me. I'll be staying in Korea for one week.
Do I need to fill out this card?

C : Yes, sir. All passengers entering Korea must fill out the ED card.
Would you like me to help you with it, sir?

P : Yes, please.

Dialogue 3

통과 여행객의 경우

C: Cabin crew(Seward/Stewardess, P: Passenger

P : I'll be at Incheon International Airport only for two hours and then I'll be flying on to Tokyo. Do I need this card?

C : No, ma'am. You don't have to fill out the card.

NOTES:

- Are you a *resident of Korea?*
  US citizen
  visitor/tourist
- Would you like me to help you with it, sir?
- All passengers entering Korea must fill out the *ED card.*
  CD form
- Do you have *a green card?*
  any fruits, animals, or plants with you
  more than US $ ________
  a U.S. visa

NOTES:

8. Destination city information(목적지 안내)

여행을 자주 하는 손님들은 자기가 가는 곳에 대해 잘 알고 있지만, 대부분의 손님은 그들이 방문하는 도시에 대한 정보를 많이 갖고 있지 않다. 그래서 그들은 목적지와 관련된 날씨, 호텔, 교통시설, 쇼핑 등에 대한 정보를 갖기를 원한다. 기내 승무원들은 이러한 손님들의 욕구를 충족시켜 주기 위해 목적지와 관련된 제반사항을 숙지하여 손님의 요청시 제공해 주어야 한다. 만일 승무원들이 제공해 줄 수 없다면 최소한 그러한 정보들이 어디에 있는지를 손님들에게 알려 주어야 한다.

한 예로, 요즈음 많은 손님들이 어떤 나라의 관광명소뿐만 아니라 그 지역에서의 쇼핑에 대해 많은 관심을 보이고 있다. 이런 경우 손님들은 아마도 환율과 은행의 위치를 알고 싶어할 것이다. 대부분의 경우 공항 내에 은행들이 위치한다는 것을 알겠지만 승무원들이 친절히 그러한 정보를 알려 준다면 매우 고마워할 것이다.

기본 어휘

accommodations	arrival time	available	climate
destination	exchange rate	terminal building	time difference
tourist desk	walking distance		

Dialogue 1   시 차

C: Cabin crew(Seward/Stewardess, P: Passenger

P : Is there any time difference between Seoul and Taipei?

C : Seoul is one hour ahead of Taipei.

P : How about between Seoul and Tokyo?

C : There's no time difference between them.

Dialogue 2 서울에 대한 정보 문의

C: Cabin crew(Seward/Stewardess, P: Passenger

P : What's the arrival time in Seoul?

C : 6:30 in the morning, ma'am.

P : How long does it take to downtown Seoul from the airport?

C : It takes about forty minutes by taxi, but it depends on the traffic. There are two kinds of taxis, the regular and deluxe.

P : Is there any bus service available?

C : Certainly, ma'am. There is an airport bus which comes every 10 minutes. It takes about one hour to downtown.

P : Thank you.

C : You're welcome. Have a nice stay in Korea.

Dialogue 3 쇼핑 문의

C: Cabin crew(Seward/Stewardess, P: Passenger

P : Do you know any good places for shopping in Seoul?

C : I would recommend Itaewon. You can get many souvenirs, inexpensive clothes, and shoes. People there can speak English.

P : I see. What else would you recommend for me?

C : Namdaemun Market is another place you can enjoy shopping. You can get everything. The items are cheap, but please make sure to bargain.

세계 시차표 / World Time Zones

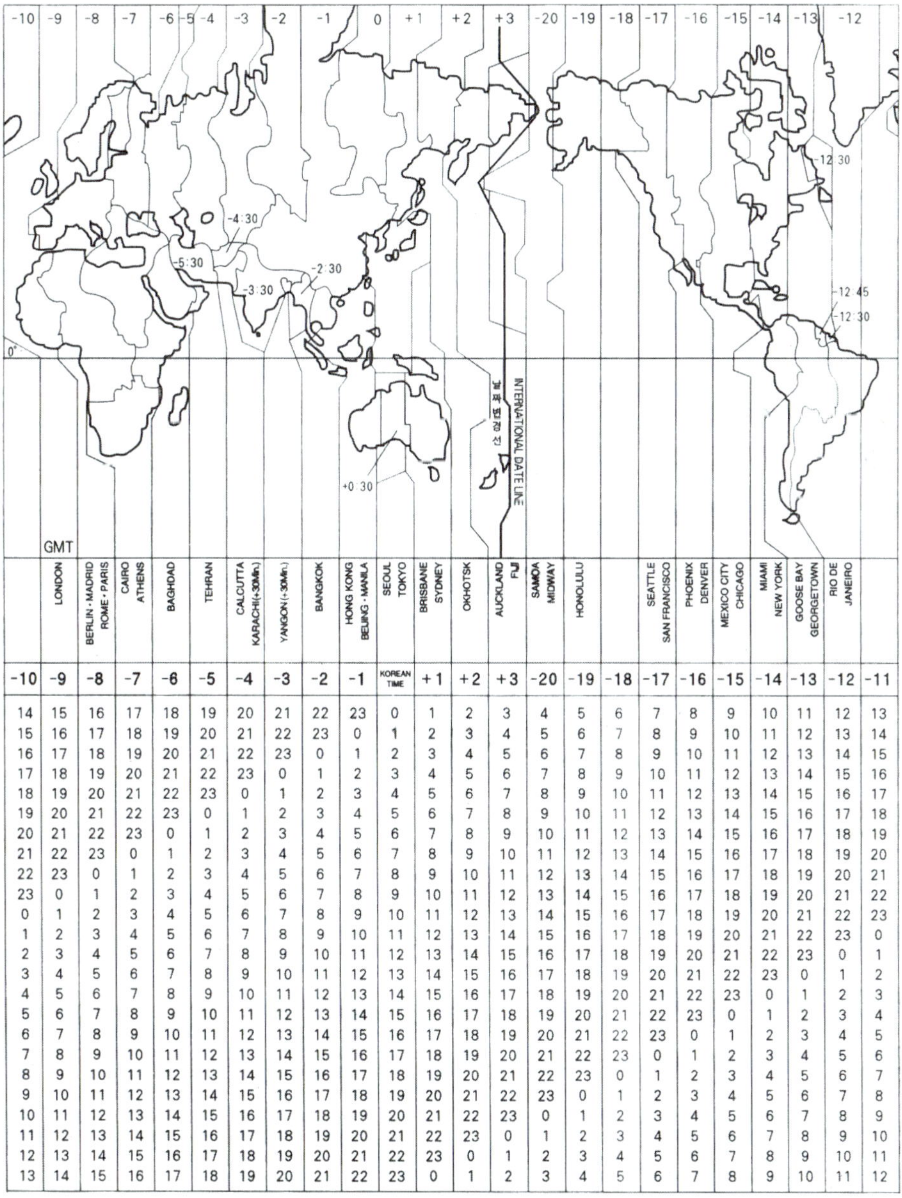

	LONDON	BERLIN · MADRID ROME · PARIS	CAIRO ATHENS	BAGHDAD	TEHRAN	CALCUTTA KARACHI(+30Min.)	YANGON (+30Min.)	BANGKOK	HONG KONG BEIJING · MANILA	SEOUL TOKYO	BRISBANE SYDNEY	OKHOTSK	AUCKLAND FIJI	SAMOA MIDWAY	HONOLULU		SEATTLE SAN FRANCISCO	PHOENIX DENVER	MEXICO CITY CHICAGO	MIAMI NEW YORK	GOOSE BAY GEORGETOWN	RIO DE JANEIRO	
-10	-9	-8	-7	-6	-5	-4	-3	-2	-1	KOREAN TIME	+1	+2	+3	-20	-19	-18	-17	-16	-15	-14	-13	-12	-11
14	15	16	17	18	19	20	21	22	23	0	1	2	3	4	5	6	7	8	9	10	11	12	13
15	16	17	18	19	20	21	22	23	0	1	2	3	4	5	6	7	8	9	10	11	12	13	14
16	17	18	19	20	21	22	23	0	1	2	3	4	5	6	7	8	9	10	11	12	13	14	15
17	18	19	20	21	22	23	0	1	2	3	4	5	6	7	8	9	10	11	12	13	14	15	16
18	19	20	21	22	23	0	1	2	3	4	5	6	7	8	9	10	11	12	13	14	15	16	17
19	20	21	22	23	0	1	2	3	4	5	6	7	8	9	10	11	12	13	14	15	16	17	18
20	21	22	23	0	1	2	3	4	5	6	7	8	9	10	11	12	13	14	15	16	17	18	19
21	22	23	0	1	2	3	4	5	6	7	8	9	10	11	12	13	14	15	16	17	18	19	20
22	23	0	1	2	3	4	5	6	7	8	9	10	11	12	13	14	15	16	17	18	19	20	21
23	0	1	2	3	4	5	6	7	8	9	10	11	12	13	14	15	16	17	18	19	20	21	22
0	1	2	3	4	5	6	7	8	9	10	11	12	13	14	15	16	17	18	19	20	21	22	23
1	2	3	4	5	6	7	8	9	10	11	12	13	14	15	16	17	18	19	20	21	22	23	0
2	3	4	5	6	7	8	9	10	11	12	13	14	15	16	17	18	19	20	21	22	23	0	1
3	4	5	6	7	8	9	10	11	12	13	14	15	16	17	18	19	20	21	22	23	0	1	2
4	5	6	7	8	9	10	11	12	13	14	15	16	17	18	19	20	21	22	23	0	1	2	3
5	6	7	8	9	10	11	12	13	14	15	16	17	18	19	20	21	22	23	0	1	2	3	4
6	7	8	9	10	11	12	13	14	15	16	17	18	19	20	21	22	23	0	1	2	3	4	5
7	8	9	10	11	12	13	14	15	16	17	18	19	20	21	22	23	0	1	2	3	4	5	6
8	9	10	11	12	13	14	15	16	17	18	19	20	21	22	23	0	1	2	3	4	5	6	7
9	10	11	12	13	14	15	16	17	18	19	20	21	22	23	0	1	2	3	4	5	6	7	8
10	11	12	13	14	15	16	17	18	19	20	21	22	23	0	1	2	3	4	5	6	7	8	9
11	12	13	14	15	16	17	18	19	20	21	22	23	0	1	2	3	4	5	6	7	8	9	10
12	13	14	15	16	17	18	19	20	21	22	23	0	1	2	3	4	5	6	7	8	9	10	11
13	14	15	16	17	18	19	20	21	22	23	0	1	2	3	4	5	6	7	8	9	10	11	12

Dialogue 4

환율과 은행에 관한 문의

C: Cabin crew(Seward/Stewardess, P: Passenger

P : I have to change some money.
Is there a bank in the terminal building?

C : Yes, the bank is on your left after you leave the customs area.

P : Can you tell me the exchange rate for US dollars?

C : I'm not quite sure. However, today's rate will be about 1,250 won to one US dollar.

P : All right, thank you.

C : You're welcome.
I hope you enjoy your stay in Korea.

Useful Expressions

- Seoul is one hour ahead of Taipei.
- There's no time difference between them.
- There is an airport bus in front of the terminal building.
- It takes about ______ minutes to downtown(the major hotels), but it depends on the traffic.
- I would recommend Itaewon. You can buy cheap clothes and shoes there.
- Today's rate is ______ won to one US dollar.
- Have a nice stay in Korea.
- I hope you enjoy your stay in Seoul.

9. Landing and deplane(착륙과 손님의 비행기 내림)

비행기 이륙 때와 달리 비행기가 착륙할 시점에는 대부분의 손님들은 제한된 공간에서 오랜 비행을 한 후이기에 매우 지쳐 있다. 오랜 비행으로 손님들은 운동이 부족하고, 때때로 소화불량 문제를 겪기도 한다. 비행기가 천천히 하강할 때에는 승무원들은 다시 한번 안전벨트 착용과 좌석의 원위치로와 tray table이 원위치로 가도록 손님들에게 당부한다. 손님들은 터미널 빌딩에 도착할 때까지 흡연이 금지되며, 통로에 있는 손님들은 제자리로 가도록 요청받게 되고, 짐들은 좌석 밑에 놓인다.

비행기가 완전히 착륙한 후에 손님들은 비행기를 내리기 시작한다. 모든 스튜어드와 스튜어디스는 문 앞을 향해 일렬로 서서 손님들에게 작별인사를 한다.

기본 어휘

deplane	descend	earphone	fall off
fall out	fasten	land	recline
refrain	seatbelt	tray table	upright

1) Before landing(착륙 전)

Dialogue 1 이어폰세트 수거

C: Cabin crew(Seward/Stewardess, P: Passenger

C : Excuse me. May I have your earphone set, please?
We'll be landing shortly. (……) Thank you, sir.
How was your flight?

P : Good. Thank you.

Dialogue 2

안전벨트 확인

C: Cabin crew(Seward/Stewardess, P: Passenger

C : Excuse me, ma'am.
Would you mind fastening your seat belt, please?
We'll be landing soon.

P : O.K.

C : Thank you.

Dialogue 3

의자 및 tray table 원위치

C: Cabin crew(Seward/Stewardess, P: Passenger

C : Excuse me. Would you mind returning your seat back to the upright position, and closing your tray table, please? We'll be landing soon.
Did you enjoy the flight?

P : Yes, I did.

C : Thank you.

Dialogue 4

복도의 손님

C: Cabin crew(Seward/Stewardess, P: Passenger

C : Excuse me, sir. Would you please return to your seat and fasten your seat belt, please?
We'll be landing shortly.

P : O.K.

C : Thank you.

Dialogue 5

짐

C: Cabin crew(Seward/Stewardess, P: Passenger

C : Excuse me. Would you mind keeping your bag under your seat, please? It might fall off during landing.

P : O.K.

C : Thank you.

Dialogue 6

컵 수거

C: Cabin crew(Seward/Stewardess, P: Passenger

C : Excuse me, sir.
Have you finished with your drink?

P : Yes, I have.

C : (taking cup away) Thank you, sir.
We'll be landing shortly. Would you mind fastening your seat belt, and closing your tray table, please?

Dialogue 7

손님의 코트나 소지품을 돌려줌

C: Cabin crew(Seward/Stewardess, P: Passenger

P : Excuse me.
Would you bring me my coat I gave it to you earlier?

C : Sure, sir. Just a moment, please.
(······)
Here is your coat, sir.
Did you enjoy our flight today?

P : Yes, it was great. Thank you.

C : You're welcome. I hope to see you on board again.

2) After landing(착륙 후)

Dialogue 1 작별인사

C: Cabin crew(Seward/Stewardess, P: Passenger

C : Good bye. Thank you for flying with us today.
See you again.

Dialogue 2 손님을 도와줌

C: Cabin crew(Seward/Stewardess, P: Passenger

C : May I help you with your bags, ma'am?

P : No, thank you.

C : (smile) Thank you for flying with us today.
Good bye. See you again.

Useful Expressions

- How was your flight?
- Would you mind *refraining from smoking,* please?
  fastening your seat belt
  returning your seat to the upright position for landing
  keeping your bag under your seat until we land
- We'll be landing shortly.
- Excuse me, sir. The no smoking sign is on.
- May I have your earphone set, please?
- Thank you for flying with us today.
- Here is your coat/bag, sir.
- I hope to see you on board again.
- I hope you enjoyed our flight today.
- Good-bye. See you again.

NOTES:

Chapter 06

En-route Announcements

기내서비스 관련 안내방송

이 장은 출발지를 떠나 목적지로 가는 과정에서 일어나는 안내방송에 관한 내용으로, 여기에는 전체적인 서비스 소개, 식음료 서비스, 영화상영, 기내 면세품 판매, 입국서류 작성 및 확인, 이어폰 수거 및 목적지 근접, 착륙, 작별 및 통과여객, 손님 하기(下機) 안내방송 등이 포함된다.

4장에서는 기내 안내방송의 일반적인 유의사항을 알아보았다. 이 장에서는 기내방송시 시간대별 특성을 고려한 유의사항을 살펴보고자 한다.

① 항공기를 자주 이용하는 비즈니스 손님이 많은 구간에서는 손님들이 기내방송에 대해 귀찮은 느낌이나 때로는 거부감까지 느낄 수 있으므로, 불필요한 정형적인(routine) 방송이나 상투적인 문구는 가급적 지양하고, 방송자가 융통성을 최대로 발휘한다. 예를 들어, 서비스방송은 삭제하고 직접 서비스를 할 수 있다.

② ①의 경우, 정형적인 방송문에 그날의 날씨, 절기, 계절에 따른 참신한 방송문을 미리 준비하여 상황에 맞는 적절한 방송으로 손님들에게 신선한 느낌을 주도록 한다. 예를 들어, '졸음이 몰려오는 봄날 오후입니다. 자칫 몸과 마음이 나른해지기 쉬운 때, 저희 ______와 함께 봄날 창공을 마음껏 날아 새로운 활력소를 불어넣는 시간이 되시기를 저희 승무원 모두는 간절히 바랍니다'라고 방송을 하면 신선한 느낌을 줄 수 있다.

③ 국내선의 경우 외국인의 탑승과 관계없이 한국어 방송에 이어 영어방송을 실시

하도록 한다.

④ 관광객이 많은 구간과 비행기를 처음 타는 손님이 많은 구간에서는 자세하고 세심하게 방송을 실시한다.

⑤ 수면을 취하는 손님이 많을 경우 기내등(cabin light)의 불빛을 줄이거나 끄고, 방송은 조용하고 부드럽게 시작하도록 한다.

1. Service plan(전체 서비스 안내)

방송

Ladies and gentlemen, we'd like to inform you of our in-flight services on today's flight to Los Angeles.

In a few minutes, we will be serving cocktails and soft drinks and followed by breakfast(lunch/dinner/a snack).

After the meal service, duty free sales will be followed, and a(two) movie(s) will be presented for your entertainment.

Two hours before arrival, breakfast(lunch/dinner/a snack) will be served.

For details of the service procedures, please refer to the in-flight magazine in your seat pocket. We wish you a pleasant flight. Thank you.

해설

손님 여러분, 로스앤젤리스까지 여러분께 제공해 드릴 기내 서비스에 대해 안내말씀 드리겠습니다.

잠시 후 칵테일을 포함한 음료서비스에 이어 아침식사를 드시겠습니다.

식사 후에는 면세품을 판매하겠으며, 이어서 한(두)편의 영화를 상영하겠습니다.

로스앤젤레스 도착 2시간 전에 간단한(음료와) 식사를 드리고, 식사 후에는 로스앤젤리스 입국에 필요한 서류를 재확인하겠습니다.

보다 자세한 내용은 좌석 앞 주머니 속에 있는 기내지를 참고하시기 바랍니다. 즐겁고 안락한 여행이 되시도록 저희 승무원들은 정성을 다하겠습니다. 감사합니다.

기내 서비스(대한항공)

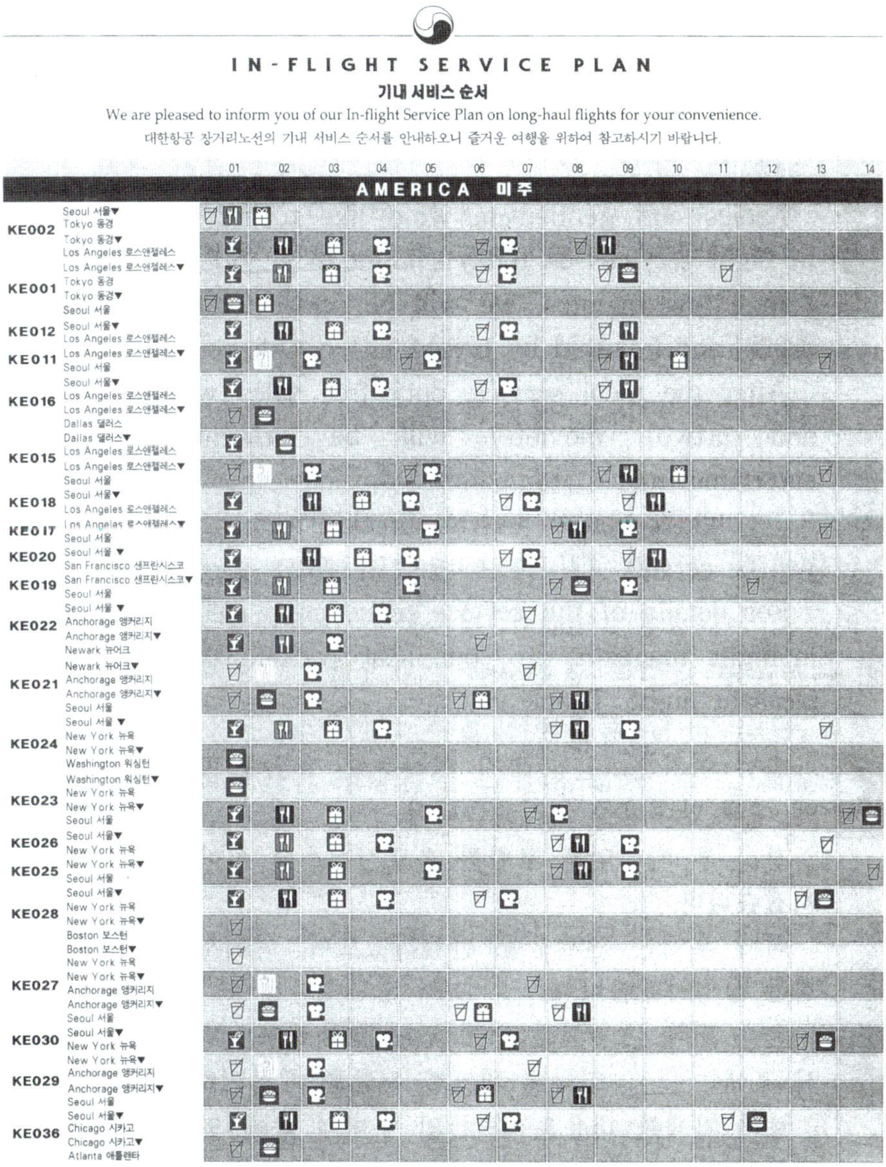

Service time and flying hours may be subject to change due to operational constraints and other unexpected occurrences.
서비스 시간 및 비행 시간은 부득이한 사정으로 변경될 수 있습니다.

2. Seatbelt sign off(좌석벨트 착용 표시등 꺼짐)

방송

Ladies and gentlemen. Although the seat belt sign has been turned off, in case of sudden turbulence, please keep your seat belt fastened at all times during the flight. We'd like to remind you that smoking is prohibited in the cabin and lavatories. Your cooperation is much appreciated. Thank you.

해설

손님 여러분, 지금부터 좌석벨트 착용 표시등이 꺼져 이동하실 수 있습니다만, 예상치 못한 기류 변화로 비행기가 갑자기 흔들릴 수 있습니다. 안전을 위해 좌석에 앉아 계실 때는 좌석벨트를 매주십시오. 그리고 기내와 화장실에서는 금연해 주십시오. 감사합니다.

3. Meal and beverage(식음료서비스)

방송

Ladies and gentlemen. Now we are flying(over 10,000 feet) to the cruising altitude. (or We are flying at cruising altitude.) Our flight attendants will be serving you cold drinks(breakfast/lunch/dinner). We wish you a pleasant flight. Thank you.

해설

손님 여러분, 이 비행기는 현재 순항고도에 진입하고 있습니다.(혹은 이 비행기는 순항고도에 진입했습니다.) 잠시 후 저희 승무원들이 음료수(아침식사, 점심식사, 저녁식사)를 제공해 드리겠습니다. 음료수로는 ____, ____ 등이 준비되어 있습니다. 즐거운 시간 되십시오. 감사합니다.

4. In-flight movie(기내 영화 상영)

방송

Ladies and gentlemen. We will be showing you a video program in a while. The video for today is ‘Sleepless in Seattle’. Thank you.

Ladies and gentlemen. We'll be commencing our in-flight movie. The title of today's feature film is 'Sleepless in Seattle,' starring Tom Hanks. Please select channel 1 for English, and channel 2 for Korean. Enjoy the movie, thank you.

해설 손님 여러분, 잠시 후 기내영화를 상영하겠습니다. 오늘 손님 여러분께 보여 드릴 비디오의 제목은 '시애틀의 잠 못 이루는 밤'입니다. 즐거운 시간이 되시기 바랍니다.

손님 여러분, 잠시 후 기내영화를 상영하겠습니다. 오늘 손님 여러분께 보여 드릴 영화제목은 톰행크스의 '시애틀의 잠 못 이루는 밤'입니다. 영어는 채널 1번, 한국어 채널은 2번에서 들으실 수 있습니다. 즐거운 시간 보내십시오. 감사합니다.

기내 서비스(아시아나 항공)

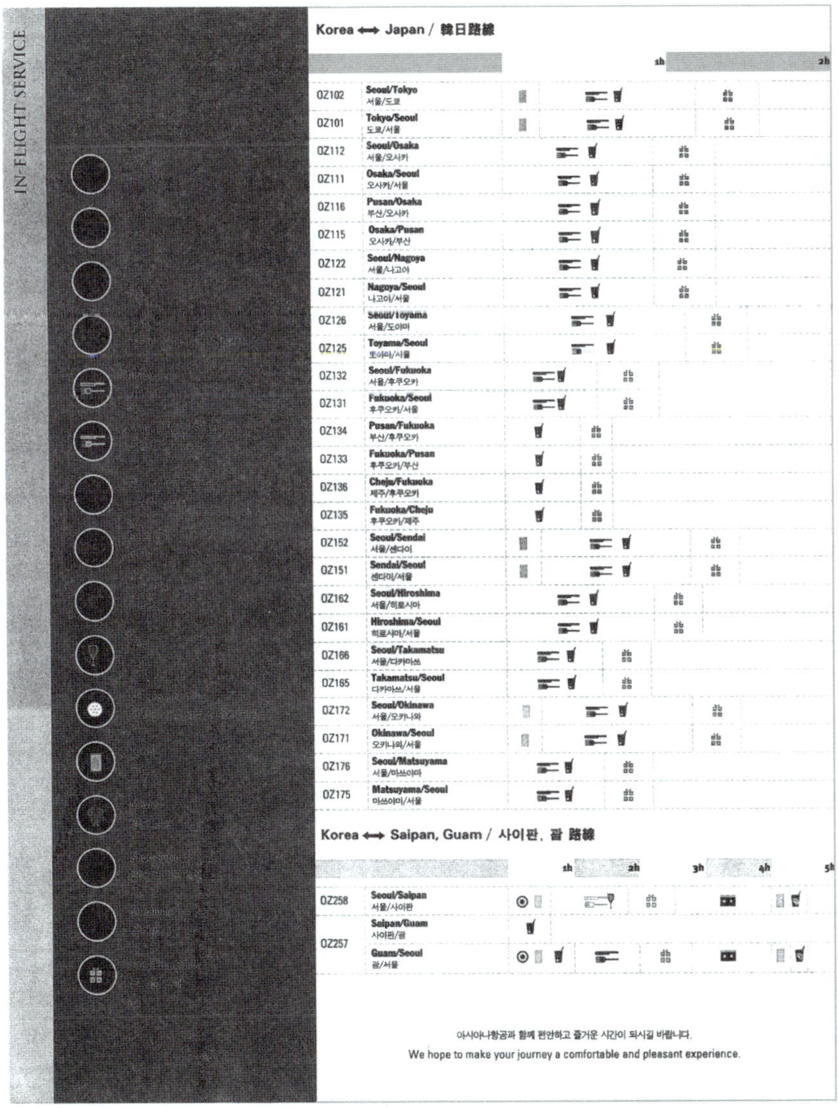

5. Turbulence(기체 흔들림)

방송

Ladies and gentlemen. This is your captain speaking. We are now having(or expect to have) some turbulence in a few minutes. So please return to your seat and fasten your seat belt. We will be out of this turbulent area in about five minutes. Thank you.

해설

손님 여러분, 본 항공기의 기장입니다. 우리 비행기는 지금(혹은 조금 후에) 기체가 흔들리고 있습니다. 약 5분 후에 이 지역을 벗어날 때까지 여러분의 좌석으로 돌아가셔서 안전벨트를 매어 주시면 감사하겠습니다.

6. In-flight duty-free sales(기내 면세품 판매)

방송

<Cart basis>

Ladies and gentlemen. In a few minutes, we'll begin our duty-free sales. If you'd like to purchase any items, please let us know as the duty free sales cart passes by your seat. For further information, please contact your flight attendants. Thank you.

<Order basis>

Ladies and gentlemen. In a few minutes, we'll begin our duty-free sales. If you'd like to purchase any items, please fill out the order form in your seat pocket and give it to your flight attendants. For further information, please contact your flight attendants. Thank you.

해설 손님여러분, 잠시 후 저희는 면세품 판매를 시작하겠습니다. 사고자 하시는 물품이 있으시면 판매수레가 여러분을 지나갈 때 저희에게 알려주시기 바랍니다. 자세한 내용은 저희 승무원에게 물어 봐 주시면 감사하겠습니다.

손님여러분, 잠시 후 저희는 면세품 판매를 시작하겠습니다. 사고자 하시는 물품이 있으시면 여러분 좌석 앞에 있는 판매주문서를 작성하시어 저희 승무원에게 전해주시기 바랍니다.

Duty-free allowances information(면세 허용량 정보)

방송

For your information, the duty free allowances for the United States are one bottle of liquor, two packs of cigarettes for visitors and four ounces of perfume.

For further information, please contact your flight attendants. Thank you.

해설 미국 국가를 여행하시는 분은 술 1병, 담배 2갑, 향수 4온스만 면세가 허용됩니다.
자세한 내용은 저히 승무원에게 물어 봐 주시면 감사하겠습니다.

7. Doctor/Nurse(응급환자 발생 및 기내 의사 호출)

방송

May I have your attention, please? we have a very sick passenger. If there's a doctor(or anyone with medical training) on board, please contact a flight attendant immediately. Thank you.

Ladies and gentlemen. Your attention, please. If there is a doctor on board, will he or she please contact a member of the cabin crew? This is a reguest for a doctor. Thank you.

해설 안내말씀 드리겠습니다. 기내에 응급환자가 발생했습니다. 의사나 간호사가 계시면 저희 승무원에게 말씀해 주십시오. 감사합니다.

손님 여러분, 잠시만 주목해 주십시오. 기내에 의사 선생님께서 탑승하고 계시면 저희 승무원에게 알려주십시오. 기내에서 의사 선생님을 찾고 있습니다.

8. Wake-up & Meal service(식사 제공)

방송

Ladies and gentlemen, we hope you've enjoyed your rest. In a few minutes, we'll be serving you lunch(or dinner/a snack/breakfast). We have one hour and twenty minutes remaining until our arrival in New York. Thank you.

Ladies and gentlemen, we'll arrive at Incheon International Airport in about one hour and thirty minutes and we'll be serving breakfast(a snack) shortly. Thank you.

해설

손님 여러분, 편안한 시간이 되셨습니까? 잠시 후 손님 여러분께 점심(저녁/스낵/아침) 식사를 제공해 드리겠습니다. 저희 비행기는 1시간 20분 후 목적지인 뉴욕공항에 도착하겠습니다.

안내말씀 드리겠습니다. 저희 비행기는 약 1시간 30뒤에 인천국제공항에 도착하겠습니다. 잠시 후 저희 승무원들이 손님 여러분께 아침 식사(스낵)을 제공해 드리겠습니다. 즐거운 시간이 되시기 바랍니다.

9. Flying over scenic spots(관광명소 통과)

방송

Ladies and gentlemen. This is your captain speaking. In a few minutes, you will be able to see Mount McKinley on the right side of the aircraft. (or We are now flying over Alaska.) Thank you.

해설

손님 여러분, 본 비행기의 기장입니다. 몇 분 후에 우리 비행기는 맥킨리산을 지날 예정입니다. 여러분의 오른쪽을 보시면 멋진 광경을 보실 수 있습니다. (혹은 우리 비행기는 알래스카를 지나고 있습니다) 감사합니다.

10. Document(입국서류 작성)

방송

Ladies and gentlemen. For entering the United States, please have your passport and other entry documents ready.

해설

손님 여러분, 미국 입국에 필요한 서류를 확인해 주시기 바랍니다.

1) Entering Korea(한국 입국)

방송

All nationalities are required to fill out both a customs form and an arrival card before entering Korea.

Passengers who have baggage arriving on another aircraft or by ship must fill out two customs forms.

After claiming your baggage at Incheon International Airport, passengers must proceed through either the green or red customs inspection lines.

Passengers not carrying items valued at more than 400 US dollars, firearms, explosives, narcotics, North Korean propaganda or articles subject to quarantine can clear customs through the green lines.

If you have more than 10,000 US dollars or the equivalent in foreign currency, you must report that amount on the customs form and pass through the red lines.

For further information, please contact your flight attendant. Thank you.

해설

입국서류는 세관 신고서와 입국 신고서(그리고 검역설문서)가 있습니다. 입국신고서는 모든 분이 작성하셔야 하며, 편명, 출발지 및 목적지를 반드시 기입하시기 바랍니다.

세관 신고서는 가족 당 1매만 작성하시면 되나, 짐을 다른 항공편이나 배편으로 부치신 분께서는 2장을 작성하시기 바랍니다. 또한 미화 10,000불 이상에 해당하는 외화를 소지하신 분께서는 세관 신고서에 신고하시기 바랍니다.

인천 국제공항 세관에서는 신속한 세관검사를 위해 여행자 휴대품 신고제도를 실시하고 있습니다.

휴대품의 해외 총 구입가격이 미화 400불 이하이고, 총포, 화약류, 마약, 동·식물의 검역물품 등을 휴대치 않은 여행자는 면세 검사대에서 신속한 세관검사를 받으실 수 있습니다.

문의사항이 있으시면 저희 승무원을 불러 주시기 바랍니다. 감사합니다.

2) Entering the United States(미국 입국)

방송

Ladies and gentlemen. For entering the United States, you'll need to have your passport and other entry documents ready. The United States government requires that an arrival card be completed by all passengers except US citizens, Canadian citizens, US green card holders, and passengers with US immigrant visas.

All nationalities must fill out the US customs form before entering the United States. Families traveling together only need to fill out one form each for their entire family.

Also, passengers having more than 10,000 US dollars or the equivalent in foreign currency or traveler's checks must declare that amount on the form.

Those passengers with connecting flights are also required to pick up all checked baggage and clear customs here in San Francisco before your next flight.

If there is any questions, please let us know. Thank you.

해설

손님 여러분, 미국 입국에 필요한 서류를 확인해 주시기 바랍니다. 입국서류는 세관신고서와 입국신고서가 있습니다.

미국 시민, 영주권 소지자, 최초 이민 손님, 캐나다 시민권 소지자를 제외한 모든 분께서는 반드시 입국 신고서를 작성하셔야 합니다.

세관 신고서는 내, 외국인 모두 작성하셔야 하며, 가족과 함께 여행하시는 손님들께서는 가족 당 1매만 작성하시면 됩니다.

그리고 손님 중에 미화 10,000불 이상 또는 이에 해당하는 외화를 지니신 분께서는 반드시 세관 신고서에 신고하시기 바랍니다.

또한 도착 후 계속해서 다른 항공편으로 여행하시는 손님께서도 반드시 이곳 샌프란시스코에서 짐을 찾아 세관 검사를 받으시기 바랍니다.

도움이 필요하시면 저의 승무원을 불러 주십시오. 감사합니다.

11. Earphone collection(이어폰 회수: Approach sign 전)

방송

Ladies and gentlemen. We are now making our final descent into Incheon International Airport. We ask you to return your seat back to the upright position, close your tray table, and fasten your seatbelt.

This includes our audio entertainment program. We hope you have enjoyed the in-flight music(and video/movie) programs. Your flight attendant will now pick up the earphones shortly. We appreciate your cooperation. Thank you.

해설

손님 여러분, 저희 비행기는 잠시 후 인천국제공항에 도착하겠습니다. 지금부터 좌석에 앉으셔서 좌석벨트를 몸에 맞도록 매주시기 바랍니다. 또한 착륙준비를 위해 손님 여러분께서 이용하신 이어폰을 회수하겠으니 협조하여 주시기 바랍니다. 감사합니다.

12. Destination approaching(목적지 접근: Approach sign 후)

1) Destination approaching(목적지 접근)

방송

Ladies and gentlemen, we are making our descent into Dulles International Airport. Please return to your seat and fasten your seat belt. Also, please turn off all electronic devices.

해설

손님 여러분, 안내말씀 드리겠습니다. 저희 비행기는 약 20분 후 덜러스 국제공항에 착륙하겠습니다. 지금부터 좌석에 앉으셔서 좌석벨트를 몸에 맞도록 매주시기 바랍니다. 어린이를 동반하신 손님께서는 유아의 좌석벨트 착용상태를 다시 한번 확인해 주시기 바랍니다. 아울러 지금 사용하고 계신 전자제품이 있으시면 전원을 꺼 주시기 바랍니다.

2) Transit passenger(경유 손님), (Approaching 방송에 이어서 방송)

(1) Passengers must remain on board.(통과여객 기내 대기시)

방송

For those passengers continuing on to Incheon, please remain seated on board. We should be on the ground for about 50 minutes.

해설

그리고 이곳 나리타공항당국의 요청에 따라 인천까지 가시는 모든 손님께서는 기내에서 대기하게 되어 있사오니 불편하시더라도 널리 양해하여 주시기 바랍니다. 이곳 나리타공항에서는 약 50분간 머물 예정입니다.

(2) All passengers must exit the aircraft.(통과여객 전원 하기시)

방송

For those passengers continuing on to Hong Kong, please exit and take a transit card. Also please take all of your belongings with you. Bags and valuables cannot be left on board. We should be on the ground for about 50 minutes. We'll make an announcement in the transit area when we're ready to reboard.

해설

이곳 나리타공항당국의 요청에 따라 홍콩까지 가시는 손님께서는 전원 내리시어 공항 내에서 대기하시도록 되어 있습니다. 내리실 때는 여권과 귀중품을 반드시 소지하시고, 그 외의 소지품은 머리 위 선반 속에 보관하여 주시기 바랍니다. 이곳 나리타공항에서는 약 50분간 머물 예정이며, 대기하시는 동안 저희 지상직원이 성심껏 모시겠습니다.

(3) Transit procedure(통과 절차)

방송

Ladies and gentlemen, for those passengers continuing on to other locations, please exit and take a transit card. Also please take your passport and valuables with you.

For those passengers with a connecting domestic flight, please pick up all checked baggage and clear customs here at Incheon International Airport. Please move to the Domestic Check-In Counter either at Incheon International Airport or at your arrival at Gimpo Airport.

When you pick up your baggage, please check that your baggage tag number and claim tag number match correctly.

Bags may be left on board if you wish but should be towed in the overhead bin. We should be on the ground for about 40 minutes. We'll make an annomcement.

Passengers with connecting international flights, please follow the guidance of our ground staff. Thank you.

해설 안내말씀 드리겠습니다. 다른 지역으로 계속 여행하시는 손님들은 비행기에서 내리셔서 통과카드를 받으시기 바랍니다. 또한 여러분들의 여권과 귀중품을 가져가시기 바랍니다.

인천국제공항 도착 후 국내선을 이용하실 분은 내리셔서 입국심사와 세관검사를 받으시고, 김포공항이나 인천 국제공항 내 국내선 탑승 수속 카운터로 이동하십시오.

위탁 수하물을 찾으실 때는 수하물 번호표를 확인하시기 바랍니다.

손님이 원하시면 가방은 기내에 놔두셔도 좋으나, 머리 위 선반 속에 보관하여 주시기 바랍니다. 우리 비행기는 이곳에서 약 40분간 머물 예정입니다.

인천국제공항에서 국제선 연결편을 이용하실 분은 내리셔서 저희 공항직원의 안내를 받으시기 바랍니다. 감사합니다.

13. Landing(착륙)

1) Example 1(예 1)

방송

Ladies and gentlemen. We are now making our final approach. Please make sure that your seatback is in the upright position, your tray table is closed, and your seatbelt is fastened. Thank you for your cooperation.

해설 손님 여러분, 저희 비행기는 곧 착륙하겠습니다. 좌석벨트 착용을 다시 한번 확인해 주시기 바랍니다. 그리고 손님 여러분의 안전을 위해, 사용하셨던 좌석 등받침과 테이블은 제자리로 해주시기 바랍니다. 감사합니다.

2) Example 2(예 2)

방송

We are now approaching Kimpo Airport in Seoul. We wish to remind you that taking pictures over the airport is strictly not permitted according to the order of Korean Government Defense Authorities. Please fasten your seat belt and remain in your seat until the plane comes to a complete stop.

해설

손님 여러분, 저희 비행기는 지금 서울 김포공항에 착륙하겠습니다. 한국 국방부령에 의해 공항을 촬영하는 것이 금지되어 있음을 다시 한번 상기시켜 드립니다. 비행기가 완전히 설 때까지 좌석벨트를 착용해 주시기 바랍니다.

14. Farewell(작별)

방송

Ladies and gentlemen. We've just landed at Incheon International Airport. The local time is 11:50 a.m.

For your safety, please remain seated with your seatbelt fastened, until we come to a complete stop and the captain turns off the seatbelt sign.

Please be sure to take all your belongings with you when you exit. And be careful when opening the overhead bins, since bags may have shifted during the flight.

On behalf of the entire flight crew, we would like to express our sincere thanks to all of you for flying Asiana airlines. We look forward to serving you again in the near future. We wish you a pleasant stay in Korea. Good-bye.

해설

손님 여러분, 방금 저희 비행기는 인천국제공항에 안전하게 도착하였으며, 이곳 현지시간은 7월 3일(오전) 11시 50분입니다.

손님 여러분의 안전을 위해 비행기가 완전히 멈춘 후 저희 승무원이 안내해 드릴 때까지 좌석에서 잠시만 기다려 주시기 바랍니다.

내리실 때는 특히 여권, 카메라, 면세품 등 잊으신 물건이 없는지 좌석주변을 잘 살펴 주십시오. 아울러 보관해두신 짐을 꺼내기 위해 선반을 여실 때는 물건이 떨어지지 않도록 각별히 유의 바랍니다.

오늘 저희 아시아나항공을 이용해 주신 여러분께 다시 한번 감사의 말씀드리며, 더욱 정성스럽고 편안하게 여러분을 모시도록 노력하겠습니다. 감사합니다. 안녕히 가십시오.

15. Deplaning(손님의 비행기 내림)

방송

Thank you for waiting, ladies and gentlemen. You may now exit through the forward door and please make sure to take all of your belongings with you when you exit. We wish you a pleasant day(evening) and thank you once again for flying Korean airlines.

해설

손님 여러분, 지금부터 앞문을 이용해 내려 주시기 바랍니다. 내리실 때는 다시 한번 잊으신 물건이 없도록 잘 살펴 주십시오. 감사합니다. 안녕히 가십시오.

PART 04

CHECK-OUT

Chapter 7 Check-out Service English
Chapter 8 Check-out Announcements

KAL LIMOUSINE INFORMATION

SEOUL Kimpo Airport ↔ Hotels

Discover The New Way to Link Your Hotel and The Airport with KAL Limousine Service.

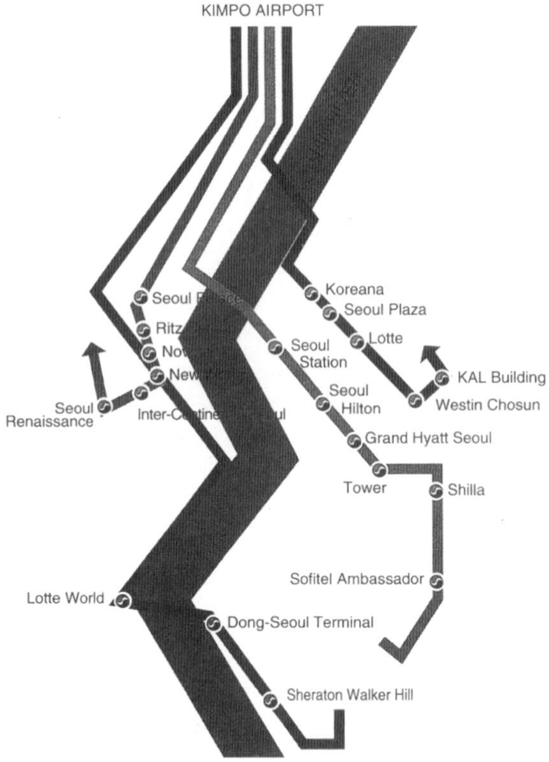

LINE 1 To/From	Koreana, Seoul Plaza, Lotte, Westin Chosun, KAL Building
LINE 2 To/From	Seoul Station, Seoul Hilton, Grand Hyatt Seoul, Tower, Shilla, Sofitel Ambassador
LINE 3 To/From	Seoul Palace, Ritz Carlton, Novotel, New World, Inter-Continental Seoul, Seoul Renaissance
LINE 4 To/From	Lotte World, Dong-Seoul Terminal, Sheraton Walker Hill

Chapter 07

Check-out Service English

입국안내 서비스 영어

손님이 비행기에서 내리면 입국심사(immigration inspection)와 세관심사(customs inspection)를 받게 된다. 손님은 입국심사대 앞의 선 밖에서 기다리다가 차례가 되면 기내에서 받은 출입국 카드(Embarkation/Disembarkation card)와 여권을 심사원에게 건네주게 된다. 입국심사관은 입국목저(purpose of visit/trip), 체류기간(length of stay), 체류지, 현금을 얼마 갖고 있는지 등을 묻는다.

입국심사를 마친 손님은 짐 찾는 곳(baggage claim)에서 자신의 짐을 찾아 세관심사(customs inspection)로 향하게 된다. 간혹 짐이 도착하지 않아 손님들이 불평하는 경우가 있으므로 항공사 직원은 손님에게 탑승권에 붙어 있는 짐표(baggage claim tag)를 받아 확인 후 짐을 찾아 주거나 혹은 짐이 다른 곳으로 가거나 출발지에서 실어지지 않았을 경우 손님에게 정중한 사과와 함께 대책을 마련해 주어야 한다.

한편, 세관직원은 신고할 물건이 있는지 없는지를 묻게 된다. 신고할 물건이 없으면 손님을 바로 입국시키고, 과세할 물건이 있으면 세관직원이 세액을 산출하여 지불용지를 작성해주어 손님으로 하여금 세금을 내고 물건을 찾아가게 한다.

기본 어휘

business	carry	destination	immigration
landing card	passport	purpose of trip(visit)	
sightseeing	stay	studying	

1. Immigration(입국절차)

Dialogue 1 입국심사 1

I: Immigration, P: Passenger

I : Good morning, sir. May I see your passport and landing card, please?
P : Sure. Here it is.
I : What's the purpose of your trip, sir?
P : Business.
I : How long do you intend to stay?
P : About three weeks at most.
I : (Stamps the passport) O.K., sir. You may go to customs now.
P : Thank you very much.

Dialogue 2 입국심사 2

I: Immigration, P: Passenger

I : Passport and landing card, please.
P : Here you are.
I : What is the purpose of your visit?
P : Sightseeing.
I : How long are you going to stay?
P : About two weeks.
I : Where are you going to stay in New York?
P : At the Hotel Hilton.
I : Thank you. Enjoy your trip, sir.
P : Thank you.

Dialogue 3

입국심사 3

I: Immigration, P: Passenger

I : What's your final destination?

P : Roanoke, Virginia.

I : What's the purpose of your trip?

P : Studying.

I : What school?

P : Virginia Tech.

I : How long are you going to stay in the United States?

P : About two years.

I : Are you carrying $ 10,000 or more with you?

P : No.

I : Thank you, sir. Enjoy your stay in the United States.

P : Thank you.

Useful Expressions

- May I see your passport and landing card, please?
- What's the purpose of your trip?
- How long are you going to stay in the United States?
- Are you carrying $10,000 or more with you?
- Where are you going to stay?
- You may go to customs now.
- Enjoy your stay in Korea.

外国人入国記録 DISEMBARKATION CARD FOR FOREIGNER ①

E.D.No. 出入国記録番号 ER 8769751　区分 21

氏 名 (漢 字) (Name)	氏 Family Name	名 Given Names	
国 籍 Nationality		生年月日 Date of Birth: Day日 Month月 Year年 19	男 1 Male　女 2 Female
住 所 Home Address		職 業 Occupation	
日本の連絡先 Address in Japan			
旅 券 番 号 Passport No.		航空機便名・船名 Flight No./Vessel	
日本滞在予定期間 Intended Length of stay in Japan		乗 機 地 Port of Embarkation	
渡 航 目 的 Purpose of visit		署 名 Signature	

官用欄 Official Use Only
外 公 通 短 一
就 特 渡 免
( )
CL/証
上特No.
入( )

官用欄 Official Use Only	S T	L N	E J	C L	S L	T P	N T	S C	O C	P P	H A	C K

カード①とカード②の太線内を入国時に記入して下さい。Please fill in CARD ① and CARD ② (inside bold line) when entering Japan.

2. Baggage claim(짐 찾기)

기본 어휘

baggage claim carrousel　　claim tag　　luggage
pick up

Dialogue 1　　짐 찾는 곳 문의 1

A: Airline agent, P: Passenger

P : Where can I pick up luggage from Asiana Flight OZ 052?

A : Carrousel 3.

P : Can you tell me where that is?

A : The one after this one.

Dialogue 2

집 찾는 곳 문의 2

A: Airline agent, P: Passenger

P : Excuse me, where is the baggage claim area?

A : It's downstairs on your right.
You can use the escalator over there.

P : Thank you.

A : You're welcome.

Useful Expressions

- Where can I pick up luggage from Asiana Flight 052?
- Where is the baggage claim area?

NOTES :

3. Baggage problems(짐과 관련된 문제)

기본 어휘

baggage claim tag	carrousel	claim
conveyor(belt) come out	contents	damage(d)
description file	fill out	lost
pay(public) phone	repair	value

1) Lost baggage(짐 분실)

Dialogue 1 짐 분실 1

A: Airline agent, P: Passenger

P : I was on United Airlines Flight 005, but my bag didn't come out on the conveyor belt.

A : Could I see your baggage claim tag?

P : Here it is.

A : Let me check on it.

(……)

Your bag was left behind in Los Angeles. It will be coming in on the next flight, which is tomorrow morning. Can you fill out this form? Description of your bag, your flight number, the value of your bag's contents.

P : Oh, yes.

A : Where are you staying?

P : I'm staying at the Hotel Shilla.

A : We'll have your bag delivered there in the morning.

Dialogue 2

집 분실 2

A: Airline agent, P: Passenger

P : Excuse me, I've been waiting for my suitcases for 40 minutes, but I can't find them.
Will you please help me to find them?

A : Sure. Do you have your baggage claim tag?

P : Yes, here you are.

A : Please wait here until I'm back. I'll try to find them.

P : Thanks, but please hurry. I have only 15 minutes left to catch a plane to go to Chicago.
(······)

A : I've located your suitcases. They were left behind in Seoul this afternoon and will arrive here tomorrow morning.

P : Oh, that's awful.
What am I supposed to do here in L.A.?

A : We are very sorry about your inconvenience. The airline will pay all expenses for you to stay in a hotel near this airport in L.A. tonight. And you can get a flight to Chicago tomorrow morning.

P : Thanks. Where can I make a long distance call?

A : There's a pay phone over there.

2) Damaged baggage(짐 훼손)

Dialogue

A: Airline agent, P: Passenger

A : What can I do for you, sir?

P : My baggage is somewhat damaged.
I'd like to have them repaired on your account.

A : We're very sorry about your inconvenience.
I will file a claim for you.

P : Thank you very much. But I'd like to have them repaired as soon as possible.

Useful Expressions

- I was on United Airlines Flight 005, but my bag didn't come out on the conveyor belt.
- Will you please help me to find my baggage?
- Could I see your baggage tag?
- Do you have your baggage claim tag?
- Let me check on it. Your bag was left behind in Seoul. It will be coming in on the next flight.
- We'll have your bag delivered there in the morning.
- My baggage is somewhat damaged. I'd like to have them repaired on your account.
- We're very sorry about your inconvenience.

NOTES:

4. Customs(세관 통과)

기본 어휘

alcoholic beverage		business	cigarette
customs	declare	declaration form	immigration
suit case	tobacco		

Dialogue 1

세관 통과 1

C: Customer officer, P: Passenger

C : May I see your customs declaration form, please?

P : Yes, here you are.

C : Do you have anything to declare?

P : No, nothing.

C : What do you have in your suitcase?

P : Just some clothes and books.

C : Would you open your suitcase, please?

P : Certainly.

C : O.K. You may go now.

P : Thank you.

Quarantine Information for the travelers into the United States.

If you are bringing fruits, meats or other agricultural commodities into the United States, you can get through inspection quicker - and avoid fines - by following a few declaration guidelines.

Fruits, Vegetables and Plants
All food items must be declared. Agricultural inspectors will examine fruits, vegetables and plants if they are free of pests or if they can be brought into the country. The fine for not declaring these items is $100 and must be paid before leaving the inspection line.

Meat and Animal Products
Fresh, dried and canned meats and meat products from most foreign countries cannot be brought into the country. There are a few exceptions, so please declare them and ask the inspectors.

Soil, Sand, Minerals and Shells
Dangerous organisms can be carried in soil or on plants. Soil, earth and sand cannot be brought into the country, although one ounce of decorative beach sand is allowed.

Agricultural inspectors are on the look out for those who may be bringing in food items without declaring them. Be safe. You should declare any of those items by checking yes on the U.S.Customs declaration card - or be prepared to pay a $100 fine.

Declare it.

Dump it.

Or pay a fine!

미국으로 입국하시는 여행객들에 대한 농산물 검역 안내

과일이나 육류 및 각종 농산물 등을 소지하고 미국으로 입국하실 경우, 아래 안내 사항 등을 준수하시면 더욱 신속하고 안전한 검역을 마치실 수 있습니다.

과일, 채소 및 각종 농산물
과일, 채소 및 각종 농산물은 반드시 사전 신고하셔야 합니다. 여러분의 입국시 검역관들은 이들 물품 등에 대한 반입 가능 여부를 심사하게 되며, 신고되지 않은 물품에 대해서는 미화 100불의 벌금이 부과됩니다.

육류 및 유제품류
미국을 제외한 다른 나라에서 생산된 각종 육류 및 유제품들의 반입은 금지되어 있습니다. 몇 가지 예외 종류도 있사오니 반드시 사전 신고하시고 검역관에게 문의바랍니다.

흙, 모래, 광물질 및 각류
위험한 유기물이 흙이나 식물류에 포함되어 운반될 수 있으니, 흙이나 모래는 반입될 수 없습니다. 그러나 장식을 위한 1온스 정도의 해안가 모래 등은 반입이 가능합니다.

검역관들은 신고없이 반입될 가능성이 있는 각종 농산물에 대해서 철저한 검역을 시행하고 있으며, 신고없이 반입되는 물품에 대해서는 미화 100불의 벌금을 부과하고 있사오니, 해당되는 물품을 소지하고 계신 승객께서는 세관신고서 작성시 반드시 신고하여 주시기 바랍니다.

Dialogue 2

세관 통과 2

C: Customer officer, P: Passenger

C : Do you have anything to declare?

P : No. I have nothing to declare.

C : Do you have any alcoholic beverages or tobacco?

P : I have some cigarettes, but just for my own use.

C : What is this?

P : They are gifts for my family.

C : You can go now.

P : Thank you.

Dialogue 3

세관 통과 3

C: Customer officer, P: Passenger

C : Do you have anything to declare, sir?

P : What kind of items do I have to declare?

C : Well, fruits, plants, animals, jewels and so on.
What do you have in this suitcase?

P : Books, clothes, shoes and some personal effects.

C : Do you have anything more besides that?

P : No.

C : All right. That's all. You may go now, sir.

P : Thank you.

Useful Expressions

- May I see your customs declaration form, please?
- Do you have anything to declare?
- What do you have in your suitcase?
- Will you open your bag, please?
- You may go now, sir.

NOTES:

5. Porter service(포터 서비스)

기본 어휘

baggage	porter	taxi stand

Dialogue

A: Airline agent, P: Passenger

A : May I help you, ma'am?

P : Yes, please. These are my bags.
Please take these to the taxi stand.

A : Very well, ma'am. How many bags do you have?

P : Three. I'll take one myself.
What's the price for each piece of baggage?

A : One dollar, please.

P : That's fair.

Useful Expressions

- May I help you?
- How many baggages do you have?
- What's the price for each piece of baggage?

6. Renting a car(렌터카)

렌터카 직원은 차를 예약한 고객이 비행기에서 내리면 바로 사용할 수 있게끔 차를 준비하고 있어야 한다. 미국의 경우 일반적인 렌트 자격은 적어도 25세가 되어야 하며, 운전면허증과 신용카드가 있어야 한다. 만약에 나이가 25세 미만이면 렌트할 수 있는 회사가 한정되며, 계약조건이 상당히 까다로워진다.

직원은 고객의 예약요청을 받으면 사용시기, 차의 종류(Economy, Compact, Intermediate(Medium), Standard, Premium, Luxury, Convertible 등), 마일리지 방식(Unlimited 혹은 Limited mileage), 보험 등을 제시하여 고객이 선택하게 한다. 여기에서 Unlimited는 하루에 몇 천 마일을 운전해도 괜찮은 것이고, Limited는 하루에 제한된 마일만을 운전해야 하며, 이를 초과할 경우에는 얼마간의 돈을 더 내야 한다. Unlimited 마일리지는 Limited 마일리지보다 렌트비가 비싸나 장거리 여행에 유리하고, Limited는 단거리 여행에 효과적이다.

참고로, 미국의 렌터카 회사의 수신자 전화번호는 다음과 같다.

Alamo	1-800-327-9633
Avis	1-800-331-1441
Budget	1-800-322-9975
Hertz	1-800-684-6511
National	1-800-328-4567
Enterprise	1-800-325-8007

기본 어휘

compact	contract	convertible	credit card
economy	insurance	coverage	intermediate
fill out	full size	inspect	late charge(fee)
limited	medium	mileage	luxury
one-way	optional	pick-up	premium
rent-a-car	rental cost	reserve	return
sedan	standard	unlimited	valid
week rate	weekend rate		

Dialogue 1

렌터카 예약 1

C: Clerk, T: Tourist

C : Good morning, may I help you?

T : Yes, I want to rent a car, please.

C : What type of car are you interested in?

T : A full size sedan.

C : We have the new Ford Taurus.

T : That sounds good.

C : When do you need it?

T : Now. How much is it?

C : Our weekend rate is $ 50 a day.
Would you like limited or unlimited miles?

T : I'd like the unlimited miles.

C : Would you like the optional insurance coverage?

T : No, thanks.

C : May I see your driver's license?

T : I have an International Driver's License.

C : That's fine. How do you want to pay?

T : Visa, please.

C : O.K. Would you sign here, and again here? (……)
Thank you. Here is your key and the car is right outside.

NOTES:

Dialogue 2

렌터카 예약 2

C: Clerk, T: Tourist

C : Hertz Rent a car. May I help you?

T : Yes, I'd like to rent a compact car tomorrow morning at 9 o'clock for about three days.

C : All right. We have a Toyota Corolla available for rent. That's the smallest thing we have right now.

T : That'll be fine. How much do you charge for that?

C : We charge $ 29.00 per day, but we'll give you 200 free miles a day. If you run over 600 miles for three days, we'll charge you 25 cents per mile.

T : I see. How about insurance?

C : If you want full insurance, it will be $ 6.00 per day.

Dialogue 3

렌터카 반환

C: Clerk, T: Tourist

T : I'm here to return the car. The car is right outside.

C : Let me inspect the car.

T : Here is the contract.

(Clerk inspects the car.)

C : Everything seems to be fine.

T : I was supposed to bring it in yesterday.

C : That's okay, but you will have to pay a late fee.

T : How much is it?

C : One day rental cost.

T : That will be fine.

Useful Expressions

- Hertz, Rent-A-Car. May I help you?
- I'd like to reserve a car, please.
- *What type* of car are you interested in?
  What size
- When *would you like it for?*
  do you need it for
- Would you like limited or unlimited miles?
- How much is it?
- May I see your driver's license?
- I'm here to return the car.

NOTES:

7. Money exchange counter(환전소)

환전소 직원은 여행객이 환전할 경우 물어보게 되는 주요 사항들, 예를 들면, 주요 통화의 환전율(exchange rate) 등을 숙지하고 있어야 한다. 또한 여행객이 여행자수표(traveler's check : T/C)를 원할 경우 T/C 사용법에 대해 자세히 설명해 주어야 한다.

T/C는 분실이나 도난을 당한 경우 즉시 재발행하여 받을 수 있지만 T/C를 살 때 T/C 사용란에 T/C 사용기록을 기재하여 T/C 사용과는 별도로 휴대하여야 한다. 사용할 때마다 귀찮더라도 수표번호와 사용한 장소(가게), 날짜 등을 만일에 대비하여 적어 두는 것이 좋다.

참고로, 영어로 지폐는 bill, 동전은 coin, 달러는 속어로 buck이라고 하며, 화폐의 속칭들은 다음과 같다.

1¢ 1센트(penny)	5¢ 5센트(nickel)
10¢ 10센트(dime)	25¢ 25센트(quarter)
50¢ 50센트(half dollar)	

기본 어휘

bill	cash	coin	currency
dime	exchange(rate)	dollar	franc
mark	money exchange	nickel	penny
pound	quarter	sign	signature
small change	traveler's check(T/C)		yen

Dialogue 1

환전 1

C: Clerk, T: Tourist

T : I'd like to change Korean won into dollars, please.

C : Sure. How much?

T : Fifty thousand won. What's the exchange rate?

C : One dollar is about 1,500 won.
Please fill out this form.

T : May I use your pen?

Dialogue 2 환전 2

C: Clerk, T: Tourist

C : May I help you, sir?
T : Please exchange this traveler's check for cash.
C : May I see your passport, please?
T : Yes, and here is the check.
C : Please sign your name here.
Now here's your money.
T : Thank you.

Dialogue 3 지폐 바꾸기

C: Clerk, T: Tourist

T : I would like to exchange $ 500.
C : How would you like it?
T : I would like two $ 50 bills and four $ 100 bills, please.
C : Here you are.
T : Thank you.

Dialogue 4 잔돈 바꾸기

C: Clerk, T: Tourist

T : Could I break two dollars into some small coins?
C : How would you like it?
T : Can I have four quarters and ten dimes, please?
C : Here you go. One, two, three, four quarters, and 1, 2, 3, 4, 5, 6, 7, 8,

9, 10 dimes.

T : Thank you.

C : You're welcome.

Useful Expressions

- I'd like to change Korean won into dollars, please?
- What's the exchange rate today?
- One dollar is about 1,500 won.
- Please fill out this form.
- How would you like it?
- May I see your passport, please?
- Here you are.

NOTES:

Chapter 08

Check-out Announcements
입국안내 관련 공항 내 안내방송

이 장은 손님이 목적지에 도착할 무렵 공항 내에서 일어나는 안내방송과 관련된 부분으로 여기에는 비행기 도착, 지연 및 결항, 임시 착륙, 습득물 분실, 손님호출 안내방송 등이 포함된다.

1. Arrival(도착)

방송

May I have your attention, please? Asiana Airlines Flight OZ 121 is now arriving from Nagoya. Thank you.

해설

마중 나오신 손님 여러분께 안내말씀 드리겠습니다. 아시아나항공 OZ 121편이 나고야로부터 지금 도착하고 있습니다. 감사합니다.

2. Paging(호출)

방송

May I have your attention, please? Mr In-soo Kim, Mr In-soo Kim, incoming passenger from Chicago, please come to the Asiana Airlines information counter.

해설 손님 여러분, 안내말씀 드리겠습니다. 시카고로부터 오신 김인수 씨, 김인수 씨, 아시아나항공 안내대로 와주시면 감사하겠습니다.

3. Arrival delayed(도착편 지연)

1) With new arrival time(새로운 도착시간 확정 안내)

방송

May I have your attention, please? We are sorry to announce that Korean Airlines Flight KE 011 from Los Angeles arriving at 12:50 will be delayed due to dense fog(heavy snow, heavy rain, strong winds). The new arrival time will be 2:30 p.m. Thank you.

해설 마중 나오신 손님 여러분께 죄송한 안내말씀 드리겠습니다. 12시 50분 도착예정이던 대한항공 로스앤젤레스로부터의 KE 011편 항공기는 짙은 안개(폭설, 폭우, 강풍)로 인하여 정시보다 1시간 40분이 지연되어 14시 30분에 도착 예정이오니 이점 널리 양해하여 주시기 바랍니다. 감사합니다.

2) Without new arrival time(새로운 도착시간 미정 안내)

방송

May I have your attention, please? We are sorry to announce that Korean Airlines Flight KE 011 from Los Angeles arriving at 12:50 will be delayed due to dense fog(heavy snow, heavy rain, strong winds). Further information will be announced as soon as possible. Thank you.

해설 마중 나오신 손님 여러분께 죄송한 안내말씀 드리겠습니다. 12시 50분 도착예정이던 대한항공 로스앤젤레스로부터의 KE 011편 항공기는 짙은 안개(폭설, 폭우, 강풍)로 인하여 정시보다 다소 지연, 도착될 예정이오니 이점 널리 양해하여 주시기 바랍니다. 정확한 도착시간은 빠른 시간 내에 알려드리겠습니다. 감사합니다.

4. Arrival cancelled(도착편 결항)

방송

May I have your attention, please? We are sorry to announce that Asiana Airlines Flight OZ 101 from Narita arriving at 12:30 has been cancelled due to dense fog(heavy snow, heavy rain, strong winds) at the Narita airport. Thank you.

해설

마중 나오신 손님 여러분께 죄송한 안내말씀 드리겠습니다. 12시 30분 도착 예정이던 아시아나항공 OZ 101편은 나리타공항의 짙은 안개(폭설, 폭우, 강풍)로 인하여 결항되겠사오니, 이 점 널리 양해하여 주시기 바랍니다. 감사합니다.

5. Divert(임시 착륙)

방송

May I have your attention, please? We are sorry to announce that Korean Airlines Flight KE 202 from Anchorage arriving at 14:20 will be diverted due to dense fog(heavy snow, heavy rain, strong winds, a technical problem, a sick passenger). The estimated time of arrival in Incheon International Airport will be 17:40 due to dense fog (heavy snow, heavy rain, strong winds). Further information will be announced as soon as possible. Thank you.

해설

마중 나오신 손님 여러분께 죄송한 안내말씀 드리겠습니다. 14시 20분 도착 예정이던 대한항공 앵커리지발 KE 202편 항공기는 짙은 안개(폭설, 폭우, 강풍, 항공기 기술상의 문제, 급한 환자)로 인하여 나리타공항에 임시 착륙할 예정입니다. 도착시간은 17시 40분 경이며, 인천국제공항으로 재운항 및 육로수송 여부는 빠른 시간 내에 알려드리겠습니다. 감사합니다.

6. Lost & Found(유실물 안내)

1) Lost(분실 안내)

방송

May I have your attention, please? Any passenger who might have a Rolex watch at the drug store, please turn it in at Asiana Airlines information counter. Thank you.

해설

안내말씀 드리겠습니다. 약국에서 로렉스 시계를 습득하신 손님께서는 아시아나항공 안내 카운터로 와 주시면 감사하겠습니다.

2) Found(습득 안내)

방송

May I have your attention, please? A Rolex watch has been found and we would like to return it to its rightful owner. The passenger who lost it, please come to the Korean Airlines information counter. Thank you.

해설

안내말씀 드리겠습니다. 대한항공에서 로렉스 시계를 보관하고 있사오니 로렉스 시계를 분실하신 손님이 계시면 대한항공 안내 카운터로 오셔서 물건을 찾아가 주시기 바랍니다. 감사합니다.

PART 05

TERMINOLOGY/ PASSENGER SERVICE

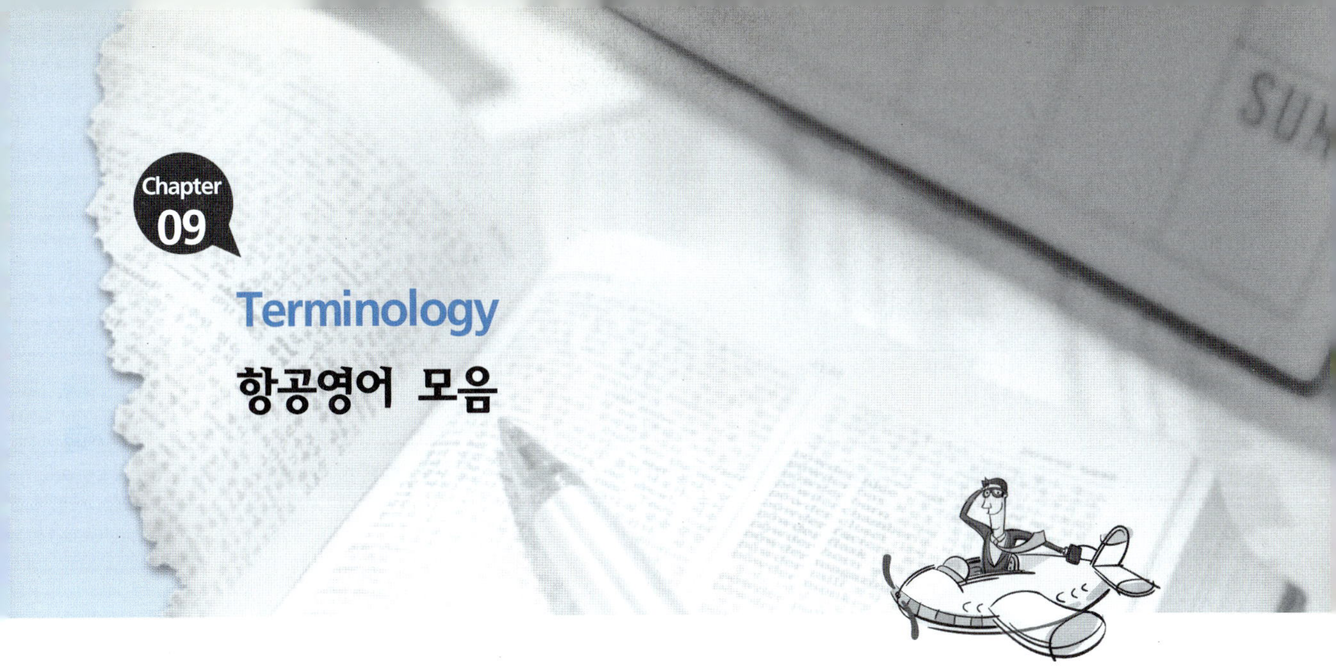

Chapter 09

Terminology
항공영어 모음

이 장에서는 위의 Part I 에서부터 Part IV까지의 전과정에서 나타나는 항공서비스 및 안내방송과 관련된 용어들을 알파벳순으로 정리하였다. 여기에는 1~8장까지 본문에서 서술된 내용과 관련된 용어 외에도 추가적인 용어들이 많이 수록되어 있어 항공사에 관심을 가진 사람들이라면 유용한 정보가 되리라 본다.

A

aboard (비행기를) 탄

accommodation 숙박(설비), 편의 제공

accompanied baggage 탁송수화물

accompanied child(minor) 12세 미만의 성인여객에 동반되는 2세 이상~12세 미만의 아이로서 요금의 50%를 할인 받음

acknowledge 인지하다

ACL(allowable cabin load) 이륙시 항공기 총중량에서 항공기 자체중량 및 연료를 제외한 유상손님과 화물을 탑재할 수 있는 최대허용량

actual flying time 실제비행시간

add 이미 예약된 사항에 추가하여 예약하는 것

adult fare 만 12세 이상 손님에게 적용되는 항공요금

advanced ticket 예매권

affinity group fare 관광 이외의 목적을 가진 단체, 법인, 협회에 소속된 경우의 특별할인

agency commission 대리점이 판매한 손님의 항공권이나 화물의 판매에 대하여 지불되는 IATA 소정의 수수료

agent 항공권판매대리점, 화물운송대리점

air cargo 항공화물

air carrier 항공사

air freight forwarder 임주로부터 화물을 접수하여 자기가 설정한 요금에 의해 항공운송을 계약함. 낱개의 화물을 집합하여 종합된 화물뭉치(대단위)를 만들어 항공사에 인도함.(=consolidator)

aircraft 항공기

aircrew 항공사 승무원

air fare 항공요금

airline counter 항공사 카운터

airline timetable 항공시간표

airlines 항공사

airlines office 항공사 사무실

airport 공항

airport bus 시내와 공항을 연결하는 버스

airport service charge 공항료

airport tax 공항세. 징수한 세금은 공항시설의 유지, 개선을 위해 쓰인다. 이는 국가별로 차이가 있으나 대략 5,000원에서 20,000원 내이다.

air bridge 공중통로

air route 항공노선

airshow 비행속도, 고도, 현지시각 및 외부온도 등 각종 운항 정보를 최신 컴퓨터

그래픽으로 제공해주는 기내 스크린서비스

airsickness 비행기 멀미

airsickness bag 구토봉투

aisle 통로

aisle seat 통로 좌석

aliens 외국인

allowance 수화물, 외환 등의 반출입 허용량

alternative airport 규정공항 착륙이 안 될 때의 교체공항

alternative reservation 손님이 희망하는 날짜의 편 이외의 예약

American Express 미국에 있는 세계에서 제일 규모가 큰 종합여행 서비스회사, 신용카드도 발행

announcement 안내방송

annual pass 타항공사의 사장, 부사장, 기타 요직에 있는 사람에 대하여 발생되는 무료우대권을 말함. 회수에 제한이 있음.

aperitif 식전수

apple juice 사과주스

application form 신청서

arm rest 팔걸이

arrival 도착(↔ departure 출발)

arrival card 입국신고서(=disembarkation)(↔ embarkation card 출국카드)

arrival record 도착기록

ash tray 재떨이(화장실 안내표지)

assistant purser 보조 사무장

assorted 여러 가지의

ATC Air Traffic Conference of America의 약어

attendant 동반자

attendant call button 승무원 호출버튼

audio service 기내용 음악감상 서비스

available 유효한, 가능한, 유용한

aviation 운항, 항공, 항해

B

baggage 수화물(=luggage). 항공기에 실려 운반되는 손님의 짐. 휴대 수화물은 hand-carry baggage, carry-on baggage, accompanied baggage, unchecked baggage

baggage allowance 수화물 중량제한

baggage cart 수화물 짐수레

baggage claim 수화물을 찾는 장소

baggage claim tag 수화물 인수증

bassinet 요람. 갓난아이를 재우기 위한 작은 상자로 예약할 때 부탁하면 기내에서 제공된다.

bay 기체와 공항의 연결 통로

behind schedule 예정보다 지연된

beverage 음료. free beverage service는 일등석에서 무료로 받을 수 있는 알코올류 서비스

beverage service 음료 서비스

blanket 담요

blind person 맹인

block time 출발지의 spot(비행기 대기 계류지점)를 출발하여 목적지의 spot에 도착하기까지의 시간으로서 시간표에 기입되어 있는 시간

board 탑승하다

boarding formalities 탑승 수속

boarding pass 탑승권

bond 보세. 입국할 때 과세대상이 되는 물품을 보세창고에 맡겨 두었다가 출국시

에 찾아갈 수 있다.

book, booking 항공권을 예약하다(=make a reservation). 항공권 예약

booklet 소책자

bound for ~행(발)

breakfast 아침식사

brunch 아침과 점심 중간의 식사

bulkhead 격벽. 첫 번째 좌석으로 요람이나 안전의자를 놓기에 충분한 공간이 있으므로 아이들을 데리고 여행하는 가족들이 자주 찾는 자리이다.

business 상용

business class 비즈니스석

business traveler 상용여행객

C

cabin 객실

cabin announcement 기내방송

cabin crew 객실승무원. 기내에서 손님의 서비스를 담당하는 사람으로서 사무장(purser), 보조사무장(assistant purser), 승무원(steward, stewardess) 등이 있다.

cabin service 기내에서의 각종 서비스

cabotage 한 국가영토 내의 상업적인 운송규제를 말함. 원칙적으로 외국항공사는 타국가 내에서의 국내구간에서 만의 운송이 금지되어 있다.

cafeteria 카페테리아, 간이식당

call button 비상용 버튼(화장실 안내 표지)

cancellation 예약취소

cancellation charge(fee) 항공권 취소료

captain 기장

car rental 자동차 대여

carrousel 손님들이 짐을 찾는 곳으로, 컨베이어벨트 위에서 짐이 빙빙 돌아간다.

carrier 항공회사

carry-on baggage 기내 휴대품

carton (담배) 갑

cash 현금

cash agent 현금교환대리점. 항공회사에서 항공권을 배포받지 못한 대리점(non-ticket holding agent)으로서 현금과 교환으로 항공권을 수령하여 손님에게 전하는 대리점

caterer 기내 물품조달자

catering 항공기에 식품류를 조달·탑재하는 것

change 잔돈

channel selector 채널선택

charge it 크레디트 카드로 결제하다

charter 대절

charter flight 대절항공기, 전세비행기

checked baggage 손님이 화물로 부치는 짐

check-in 탑승 수속. 손님이 항공사 카운터에서 항공권, 여권, 비자 및 위탁수화물에 대한 수속을 하고 좌석번호를 지정한 탑승권을 받기까지의 수속과정을 말한다.

check-in counter 탑승 수속구

check-out 입국수속

chief purser 수석사무장

children fare 아동요금으로 만 2세 이상 12세 미만의 어린이에게 적용되며, 성인요금의 80%를 지불하고 좌석배정을 받으며, 화물허용기준도 성인과 똑같이 적용된다.

chiller 기내 작은 냉장고

choice 선택

cigar 여송연

cigarettes 담배

CIQ Customs, Immigration, Quarantine(세관검사, 출입국수속, 검역)

circle trip 출발지와 도착지가 동일지점으로 항로가 중복되지 않고 돌아오는 일주 관광

circular 회람용 인쇄물

citizenship 시민권

city call 시내전화(=local call)

city excursion(tour) 시내관광

city terminal 시내 항공터미널

Civil Aviation Bureau(CAB) 민간항공국

claim tag 탁송하물 인환증

cleaner 청소요원

clearance 통관수속, 입국허가, 비행허가

client 고객

climate 기후, 날씨

clockroom 옷을 걸 수 있는 기내 캐비닛

coach class 미국 국내항공에서 쓰이는 말로 2등석을 가리킨다.

cockpit 조정실

cockpit crew 항공기의 운항을 책임지고 있는 운항승무원. 기장(captain), 부조종사(co-pilot), 항공사(navigator), 항공기관사(flight engineer)로 구분된다.

coffee 커피

coke 콜라

collect call 수신자부담 전화

commercial communications 상업통신시설

commercially important person(CIP) 항공사와 중요한 관계를 맺고 있는 업체의 고위 간부

communication network 통신망

compartment 갤리 내 기내 서비스용품을 넣어 두는 곳

complaint 불평, 불만

complimentary service certificate 무료봉사증명서

concourse 출입국하거나 세관 검사장으로 가는 좁은 통로

conditional stopover 조건부 도중체류

conditions of carriage(COACT) 운송약관, 항공권 발행에 의하여 손님과 항공사 간에 체결한 계약

conference 회의

confirm 예약을 확인하다(reconfirm은 예약을 재확인하다.)

confirmation 예약확인

conjunction ticket 한 권의 항공권에 기입 가능한 구간은 4개 구간이므로 그 이상의 공간을 여행할 때에는 한 권 이상의 항공권으로 분할하여 기입한다. 이들은 일련의 항공권을 말하며, 각각의 항공권면상에 타의 번호를 기입한다.

connecting flight 연결편 비행기

connecting time interval 최소연결 필요시간(minimum connecting time). 이것은 각 공항마다 다르므로 final release OAG를 참고하여 일정을 작성하여야 한다.

consul, consulate 영사, 영사관

contact address 연락처

continuing itinerary 여행일정이 두 개의 도시로 끝나는 것이 아니고 제3, 제4로 이어지는 것

control tower 공항관제탑

copilot 부조종사

cordless phone 무선전화기

cosmetics 화장품

credit card 신용카드

crew 승무원

crew bunk 승무원들을 위해 마련한 침상

crew certificate 국제항공협회가 인정하는 비상사태에 관한 승무원 자격증

crew seat 운항승무원석

CRT Cathode Ray Tube의 약자로 컴퓨터에 연결되어 있는 전산장비의 일종으로 TV와 같은 화면과 자판으로 구성되어 있으며 메인 컴퓨터에 저장되어 있는 정보를 즉시 보여주거나 필요시 출력도 할 수 있다.

cruising 일정고도, 3만 3천 피트로 순항하는 것

currency 통화

currency declaration 통화신고

customs 세관

customs clearance 통관절차

customs declaration form 여행자 휴대품 신고서

customs inspection 세관검사

customs officer 세관원

D

date of birth 생년월일

date of issue 발행일

day excursion 당일여행(=day tour)

daylight saving time 여름에 시간을 1시간 빠르게 하는 것(=summer time)

DBC(Denied Boarding Compensation) 보상금. 초과예약이 되어서 손님이 예정된 시간에 탑승을 못하는 경우 항공사 측에서 숙박비나 관광비용 등을 지불해주는 일종의 보상금이다.

DCS(Departure Control System) 공항에서의 손님의 탑승 수속 및 탑승관리업무의 전산화시스템

declaration of indemnity(Letter of Indemnity) 동반자 없는 소아 손님, 환자, 기타 면책사항에 관해 항공상에 만일의 경우에도 책임을 묻지 않는다는 요지를 기입한 보증서

declare (세관에서 과세품을) 신고하다.

delay 비행기의 출발, 도착이 지연되다.

depart, departure 출발하다, 출발(↔ arrival 도착)

departure record 출발기록

departure time 출발시간

deplaning point 항공기에서 내리는 지점(공항)

deportee 추방

deposit 예치금

destination 목적지

diaper 유아용 기저귀

dinner 저녁식사

direct flight 직항편(=nonstop flight)

direct sales 타 항공사나 대리점을 통하지 않고 자사에서 직접 판매하는 것

discount fare 할인요금

disembarkation card 입국카드(=arrival card) (↔ embarkation card 출국카드)

dispatcher 운항관리사. 항공기의 안전운항을 확보하기 위하여 사전에 지상조건이나 비행경로상의 제 운항정보를 채집하여 비행계획을 수립하여 기장의 합의를 받는다. 비행 중에는 항공기의 위치통보를 지켜보면서 운항사항을 파악하고 비행의 종료에 이르기까지 안전운항을 위한 하늘과 육지의 연결역할을 한다.

disturb 방해하다, 교란하다, 잠을 깨우다

divert 항공기가 기상 및 제반 여건에 의해 예정 공항에 착륙하지 못하고 인근의 다른 공항에 착륙하는 것

divide one transaction 여러 명의 손님이 예약되어 있는 경우 그 가운데 한 명

또는 다수를 분리해 내는 경우

domestic flight 국내선(=domestic service)

double booking 이중 예약

down grade 상급등급에서 하위등급으로 변경하는 것

DSR(Daily Sales Report) 항공권 판매에 관한 일일 판매보고서

duration 여행기간, 기간

duplicate reservation 동일의 손님이 동일 노선에 1회의 여행에 대하여 두 번 이상으로 중복하여 예약하는 것

duty free allowance 면세로 반출입할 수 있는 양

duty free sales 면세품 판매

duty free shop 면세점

E

earphone 이어폰

economy class 항공기의 2등석

embarkation 승선

embarkation card(E/D card) 출국카드(↔ disembarkation card 입국카드)

emergency 비상사태

emergency exit 비상구

emergency instruction 비상사태 행동설명

emergency instructor 비상사태와 응급치료에 관한 교육을 담당하는 강사

emergency landing 비상착륙

emergency note 비상사태시 행동요령이 기록된 노트

endorsement 타 항공기로의 항공권 양도

engine trouble 엔진고장

entree 주요리

equipment 각종 장비, 기계

E.T.A. 도착예정시간(Estimated time of arrival)

E.T.D. 출발예정시간(Estimated time of departure)

excess baggage 무료휴대수화물 허용량을 초과하는 수화물

exchange rate 환율

extra charge 초과요금

extra flight 임시편, 특별편

extra weight 초과중량

excess 무료 수화물 허용초과

excursion 1~2일의 짧은 여행인데, 항공용어에서는 주유여행을 말하며 이것에 적용되는 것이 excursion fare이며 할인요금의 일종이다.

eye mask 수면을 위한 눈가리개

F

family name 성(姓)

fasten your seat belt 좌석벨트를 매어주십시오.

faucet 수도꼭지

female 여자, 여성(의)(↔male 남자, 남성(의))

fill in 기입하다

fill out 기재하다

fire extinguisher 소화기

First Aid 비상약

first available flight 가장 먼저 연결 가능한 항공편

first class 일등석

first name 이름(=given name)

FIT 개인 여행객(Foreign Independent Tourist)

flight attendant 승무원

flight board 운항게시판

flight coupon 항공권의 일부로서 손님이 탑승하는 구간을 표시한 것이며, 탑승 수속시 공항에서 탑승권과 교환함

flight engineer 항공기관사

flight number 비행기 편명

flight schedule 비행계획

flight time 비행시간

flush toilet 사용 후는 물로 씻어 주세요(화장실 안내표지)

flying hours 비행시간

FNPL 항공운임 후불제도(fly now pay later)

food cart 기내식을 옮기는 운반 수레

for sightseeing 관광으로

forced landing 비상착륙, 불시착

form of payment 지불수단(현금, 수표 등)

formality 수속, 절차

fragile 깨지기 쉬운

freight(er) 화물운송(기)

frequency 운항횟수, 운항빈도

frequent flyer program 상용고객우대제도

full 좌석이 만석인

G

galley (비행기 안의) 취사실

gate lounge 탑승구 대합실

gate number 탑승구 번호

get off, get on 내리다, 탑승하다

gift 선물

gift shop 선물가게

GIT 단체여행객(Group Inclusive Tour)

given name 이름(=first name)

GMT(Greenwich Mean Time) 영국의 그리니치 천문대의 세계 표준시(정오 12시)

go-show stand by라고도 하며, 미리 예약을 하지 못한 손님이 남은 좌석이 생기면 탑승하려고 공항에 나와서 기다리는 것

government formalities 출입국 절차(=Customs, Immigration, Quarantine; CIQ)

green card 영주권

green channel 면세검사대

grooming 화장, 몸차림

grooming room 화장하는 방

ground arrangement 여행자가 목적지에 도착한 후 서비스하는 제반사항(식사, 숙박, 지상교통 등)

ground service 이륙 전 신문, 헤드폰, 타월, 음료수 등을 서비스하는 것

ground staff 지상근무요원

GSA(general sales agent) 총판매 대리점. 판매증진을 위한 계약형태의 일종으로 어떤 항공사를 위해 일정한 지역의 판매를 총괄하도록 지정되며 판매액에 대한 수수료를 받는다.

guarantee 보증

guaranteed day-off 비행 사이사이 쉬는 날

guide 안내원

guide tour 안내원이 인솔하는 여행

H

hand towels only 화장지 이외는 버리지 마세요(화장실 안내표지)

headphone jack 헤드폰 잭

high season 성수기

hijack(er) 비행기 납치(납치범)

hospitality 환대, 친절한 접대

I

IATA 국제항공운송협회(International Air Transport Association)

ICAO 국제민간항공기구(International Civil Aviation Organization)

identification card 신분증

immigration 이민, 입국심사(=passport control)

immigration office 이민국

immigration officer 이민국 관리(官吏)

impose a duty 관세를 부과하다

inaugural flight 처음 취항하거나 노선을 개설할 때 처음 띄우는 항공편

inbound 외국인의 한국여행의(↔outbound 한국인의 외국여행)

incoming passenger 입국손님(↔outgoing passenger 출국손님)

inconvenience 불편

infant 2세 미만의 유아

infant fare 유아요금으로 만 2세 미만의 아기의 경우 성인요금의 10%가 적용되며, 좌석배정이 없고 유아용품 이외엔 어떤 화물도 허용되지 않는다.

inflight 기내의, 비행중의

inflight announcement 기내안내방송

inflight magazine 기내잡지

inflight meal 기내식사

inflight movie 기내영화

inflight sales 기내면세품의 판매

inflight service 기내서비스

information center(desk) 안내소

inspection of plants 식물검사

instructor 지도교사

international airport 국제공항

international terminal 국제선

issue a ticket 발권하다

itinerary 여행일정표, 여정(표)

J

jet lag 여러 시간대를 옮겨 다닐 때 나타나는 신체의 시차 부적응 현상으로 시간이 경과하면 자연히 치료가 되지만 증상이 심할 경우를 대비하여 출발 전에 수면시간을 목적지의 시간대에 맞춰 조금씩 조절하는 것이 좋다.

jet stream 제트기류. 지구상의 중위고도 상공을 일정 방향으로 강하게 부는 바람

jewelry 보석류

jug 물주전자

juice 주스

jump seat 조종석 내 잔여석으로 기장의 허락 하에 영어로 의사소통이 가능한 손님에게 배정된다.

junior crew 신입승무원

K

kit 한 세트, 팩, 박스

Korean City Air Terminal(KCAT) 도심공항터미널로 삼성동 무역센터에 위치하며 항공권발매, 탑승 수속과 수화물 운송서비스, 김포공항과 도심공항터미널 간의 직행 리무진버스 서비스를 한다.

L

land, landing 착륙하다, 착륙(↔take-off 이륙)

landing gear 착륙기어

latitude 위도

lavatory 화장실

layover 직행 항공편이 없어 가장 빠른 연결편을 탑승할 때까지 기다리는 것

leave 출발하다, 떠나다, 남겨두다

life boat 구명보트

life demonstration 구명조끼, 산소마스크 사용법 등의 비상사태시의 행동에 대해 승무원이 직접 해 보이는 시범

life jacket/vest 구명조끼

lift 승강기(~로 들어올리다, ~를 태워주다)

light button 독서등 버튼

light switch 표시등

limousine 리무진. 공항과 시내 간을 운항하는 정기운행 버스

liner 정기운항 항공기

liquor 주류

load factor 전체 좌석과 손님 수와의 비율(즉, 좌석 이용률)

local boarding passenger 중간기착지에서 탑승하는 여객

local call 시내전화(=city call)

local time 현지시간(=zone time). GMT(그리니치 표준시)와의 시차가 있음

long distance call 장거리 전화

Lost & Found 공항에 있는 유실물 취급소

low hill 상공에서 신는 굽 낮은 구두

low season 비수기

luggage 화물(英) (=baggage 화물(美))

lunch 점심식사

M

mach 마하, 음속

maintenance (항공기, 기계 등의) 정비

male 남자, 남성(의)(↔female 여자, 여성(의))

MCO(miscellaneous charges order) 항공요금 및 관련요금의 지불증으로서 항공사 간 자기앞수표 같은 기능을 발휘하여 항공여행 제경비를 지불할 수 있는 제지불증명수표

meal service 식사서비스

medicine 약

medium 중간의, (고기 등) 중간정도로 익힌

meeting (공항 등에서의) 영접

meeting service 공항에서의 출영서비스(↔sending service 환송서비스)

minimum connection time 항공기를 갈아타기 위한 최소한의 필요시간

misconnection 연결비행편이 있을 때 비행기를 갈아타야 할 지점까지 운송하는 항공편이 연착하거나 결항하여 예정된 편에 연결되지 못하는 것

mock-up 실물크기의 항공기 모형

money exchange 환전

money exchange counter 환전소

N

NASA 미국항공우주국(National Aeronautics and Space Administration)

national carrier 국적기

nationality 국적

navigator 항공사

news stand 신문대

night shift 야근

no cigarette disposal 꽁초를 넣지 마시오(화장실내 안내 표지)

no record(NRD) 손님이 탑승 수속시 확약된 티켓을 제시했으나, 항공사 쪽에는 예약을 받은 기록이나 좌석을 확약해 준 근거가 없는 상황을 말함

no show 예약을 하고 제시간에 도착하지 않거나 아예 나타나지 않은 손님

no smoking in toilet 화장실 내에서는 금연(화장실 내 안내 표지)

no smoking sign 금연등

no smoking zone 금연구역

nonstop 직행(=direct)

non-smoking(section) 금연(구역)(↔ Smoking section 흡연구역)

normal fare 정상요금

NOSUB(not subject to load) 무임 혹은 할인요금 손님이지만, 일반유상 손님과 동일하게 좌석예약의 확보가 되는 것

not for drinking 먹는 물이 아닙니다(화장실 내 안내 표지)

not for dental purposes 양치질용으로 쓸 수 없습니다(화장실 내 안내 표지)

NOTAM(notice to airman) 항공정보. 항공의 제시설, 업무, 방식 또는 위험 등의 설정상황 조건의 변경에 관한 것으로 운항관계자에게 지체없이 통보되는 고지사항

O

occupation 직업

occupied (기내화장실) 사용중 (↔ vacant 비어 있는)

off season 비수기(↔ on season 성수기)

off shoulder 비수기

Official Airline Guide(OAG) 세계항공시각표

on board ~을 탑승한

on business 사업차

on-line/off-line on-line은 우리 항공기가 정기 운항되고 있는 노선(도시)을,

off-line은 반대로 우리 항공기가 정기적으로 운항되고 있지 않은 노선(도시)을 나타낸다. 일반적으로 다른 단어와 연합되어 사용된다.

예) on-line fare, off-line station 등

on season 성수기(↔ off season 비수기)

on time 정각에

open ticket 아직 구체적으로 날짜가 기재되어 있지 않은 항공권으로 손님이 나중에 예약을 하여 자리를 확보한 후 탑승할 수 있다.

operation 운항, 운영, 영업, 운전

orange juice 오렌지주스

origin 최초 출발지

outbound 한국인의 외국여행의(↔ inbound 외국인의 한국여행의)

outgoing passenger 출국손님(↔ incoming passenger 입국손님)

overbooking 초과예약. 항공기에 탑승할 수 있는 정원보다 더 많이(약 120%) 예약을 받아놓은 상태로서 이는 IATA에서 공식적으로 인정해 주고 있다.

overhaul 항공정비의 최종단계로서 엔진 또는 장비품을 기체에서 장탈하여 정비공정에서 분해 검사한 후 불량한 것을 교환 또는 수리한 후 재조립하여 사용가능 상태로 만드는 과정

overhead bin 머리 위의 선반(=overhead shelf)

overhead compartment 머리 위 짐칸

overhead locker 천장 밑, 짐을 넣는 공간

overhead shelf 머리 위 선반(=overhead bin)

overnight bag 여행가방

oxygen mask 산소마스크

P

paging service 호출 서비스

paid 완불한

paper cup 종이컵

paper towel 종이타월

passenger 손님

passenger list 손님명단

passenger ticket 항공권

passport 여권

passport control 입국심사(=immigration)

passport number 여권번호

pax passenger, 즉 손님을 줄여서 부르는 말

pay(public) phone 공중전화

peak season 최고 성수기

period of stay 체류기간

perfume 향수

permanent address 본적

personal belongings(effects) 소지용품

pillow 베개

pilot 비행기 기장

pitch 발을 뻗을 수 있는 공간의 크기. 특히 앞좌석을 뒤로 눕혔을 때 가슴을 펼 수 있는 공간의 크기를 나타내는 단위로서, 앞좌석의 등받이로부터 자기 좌석의 등받이 앞부분까지를 말한다.

place of birth 출생지

please lock door 문은 잠가 주세요(화장실 안내표지)

PNR(passenger name record) 예약기록, 즉 손님의 이름, 여정별 모든 예약상황, 전화번호 등 해당손님에 대한 제반 예약상황 및 서비스사항에 관한 기록

port of arrival 출발지

port of departure 도착지

porter 짐꾼(=redcap)

prepaid 선불의

presentation 상영, 상연, 증여, 선물

profession 직업

prohibited article 반입금지품

PTA(prepaid ticket advice) 항공운임의 선불제도(송금제도)로서 운임 지불인이 멀리 떨어져 있는 여객을 위하여 운임을 불입하고, 실제로 탑승할 손님이 있는 곳에서 발권을 하여 손님에게 항공권을 전해 주도록 통지하는 것

purpose of visit 방문목적

purser 사무장

push button 버튼을 누르시오(화장실 안내표지)

put out (담뱃불을) 끄다

Q

quarantine 검역

quarantine office 검역소

quotation 견적

R

ramp 연결통로

ramp-out(in) 항공기가 공항의 활주로 부근의 계류장(ramp)에 체류되어 있는 상태에서 출항을 하기 위하여 바퀴가 움직이기 시작하는 상태를 ramp-out이라 한다. 입항하는 항공기가 활주로를 벗어나 일정한 계류지점(spot)에 계류하기 위하여 정지한 것을 ramp-in이라 한다.

reading light 독서등

reclining button 등받이 버튼

recommendation 추천

reconfirm 예약을 재확인하다

reconfirmation 예약 재확인

red channel 과세검사대

re-entry 재입국

refill 보충하다

refrain 삼가다

refreshment 간식

refund 환불(하다)

register 등록하다

registered mail 등기우편

regular rate 정상기본요금

regular service 정기운항편

reimburse 갚다, 배상하다

reissue 이미 항공권을 여정 변경, 항공사 변경, 좌석등급 변경 등의 사유로 차액을 징수 혹은 지불하여 재발권 해주는 것

request 요청·신청(하다)

reservation 예약

reservation clerk 예약계

reservation control 예약조정

reservation status 예약상황

residents 거주자

rest room 화장실

return to seat 좌석으로 돌아가시오(화장실내의 안내 표지)

roster 비행 스케줄

round ticket 왕복티켓(↔ one-way ticket 편도티켓)

row 열, 줄

S

safety 안전

sanitary-napkin 생리용품

scale 저울

schedule 운항계획(시간표)

schedule board 발착일람표

seat assignment 좌석배정

seat configuration 좌석배치

seat belt 좌석벨트

seat belt sign 좌석벨트에 관한 지시등

seatfone 좌석등받이 뒤에 부착되어 있는 전화기로 신용카드로 사용한다.

seat number 좌석번호

seat pocket 좌석 주머니

seat reclining button 좌석등받이 조절버튼

section leader 좌석의 각 지역을 책임지고 담당하는 승무원

security check 기내에 위험물을 갖고 들어가는 것을 막기 위해 탑승 전에 행하는 신체·화물 검사

security check point 공중납치인 하이잭(hijack) 방지를 위한 체크 포인트(=walk through gate)

sending service 공항에서의 환송서비스(↔ meeting service 출영서비스)

senior purser 선임 사무장

separate 떼어놓다, 분리하다, 헤어지다

service flow 서비스 순서

shaver outlet 전기면도기꽂이(화장실 안내표지)

shift 교대근무

shuttle service 공항 내 순환버스

shoulder 비수기도 성수기도 아닌 과도기적 시기

signature 서명

sightseeing 관광

silent review 비상착륙시 기체 탈출의 순서를 외는 것

sky shop 기내 면세점

smock 기내 작업용 앞치마

smoking section(zone) 흡연(구역) (↔ Non-smoking section (zone) 금연구역)

snack 스낵

soap 비누

soft drink 청량음료수

souvenir 기념품

souvenir shop 기념품점

spill (물 등을) 쏟다

spot 이·착륙을 위해 비행기가 대기하는 계류지점

SST(Super Sonic Transport) 초음속제트기

stand by 예약하지 않고 공항에서 좌석이 나기를 기다리는 것

steward 남자승무원

stewardess 여자승무원

sticker 불요불급한 항공권의 재발급을 피하는 방법으로, 항공권상의 예약상황을 변경하는데 사용하는 조그마한 딱지

stopover 항공사와의 사전 약정 하에 손님이 여행 중 기착지에서 체류함

SUBLO(subject to load) 사전에 예약이 인정되지 않고 여객이 있을 때 탑승할 수 있는 손님. 예를 들어, 무임 혹은 할인요금으로 탑승하는 항공회사 직원 등이 있다.

supper 저녁식사

swap form 비행스케줄 교환을 요청하는 서식

T

take-off 착륙 (↔ landing 이륙)

tariff 항공여객 운임이나 화물요금 및 그들의 관련규정을 수록해 놓은 운임표

tax-free article 면세품

taxing 지면을 활주하는

tea 홍차

temperature 온도

terminal building 공항청사

the international date line 국제 날짜변경선

the plane for Seoul 서울행 비행기

ticket booth 매표소

ticketing 발권업무

ticketing time limit 예약신청 후 혹은 출국 전 일정시점까지 항공권을 구입하도록 되어 있는 항공권 구입시한

TIM(travel information manual) 손님이 해외여행시 필요한 정보, 즉 여권, 비자, 예방접종, 세관관계 등 각국에서 요구하는 규정이 알파벳순(국가순)으로 수록되어 있는 소책자

time difference 시차

timetable 운항시각표

toilet 화장실

toilet flushing control 수세식변기 스위치

toilet paper 화장지(=toilet tissue)

toilet seat cover 화장실 깔개

toilet seat 변기

tomato juice 토마토 주스

touch-down 기체가 활주로에 착륙을 시도하는 것

tourist information 관광안내소

towel 수건

towel disposal 쓰레기통(화장실 안내표지)

traffic 운송, 교통

traffic right 운항권

transfer 갈아타기

transfer ticket 갈아탈 수 있는 표

transit 통과

transit passenger 통과여객

transit pass(card) 통과패스

transit room 통과여객의 대합실

travel agent 여행사

travel documents 여행구비서류

traveler aid 여행자 안내소(=Information)

traveler 여행자

traveler's check(T/C) 여행자 수표

tray table 기내에서 식기를 놓는 탁자

trainee 수습승무원

trip pass 무임우대탑승권

through check-in 단일항공권으로 여정이 끝나지 않고 접속항공편을 가지고 있는 손님의 경우(통상 24시간 이내) 수화물을 최종 항공편의 목적지까지 부치는 것

turbulence 난기류

TWOV(transit without visa) 손님이 제3국으로 여행하기 위하여(비행기를 바꿔 탈 목적) 일정 조건하에서 비자 없이 입국하는 것

U

unchecked baggage 기내 휴대수화물

unload 화물을 내리다

upgrade 예약 클래스보다 위 클래스로 탑승하는 것(↔ downgrade)

upright 직립의, 똑바로, 수직으로

urgent 긴급한

used blades 다 쓴 면도날은 이곳에(화장실 안내표지)

V

vacant 기내 화장실이 비어 있는(↔ occupied 사용 중)

vaccination certificate 예방접종증명서(=yellow card)

valid 유효한

validate 항공권 등의 발효를 표시하기 위하여 기계적으로 stamping하는 것

valuables 귀중품

vending machine 자동판매기

ventilation 통풍

VIP room 귀빈실

visa 입국사증

visa application 비자신청

volume control 음량조절

voucher 증명서, 보증서

W

waiting 예약이 만원이 된 상태에서 누군가의 취소를 기다리고 있는 상태

waiting list 대기자 명단

waiting room(lounge) 대합실, 대기실

walk through gate 보안체크 포인트(=security check point)

waste chute 휴지통

weather bureau 기상대

weather map 기상도

welcome aboard 탑승을 환영합니다.

window 창문

window seat 창문쪽 좌석

X

X-ray 수화물 투시검색장비

Y

yellow card 예방접종 증명서(=vaccination certificate)

youth fare 학생할인(=student discount)

Z

zone time 지방시각, 현지시각(=local time)

Chapter 10

Passenger Service
손님 응대

1. 손님의 욕구

1) 배고픔 및 갈증에서 벗어나려는 욕구

인간의 가장 기본적인 욕구 중의 하나는 생명을 연장, 보전시켜 주는 음식물 섭취이다. 그러므로 기내 서비스에 있어서도 가장 기본이 되는 것은 음식물 서비스이다. 따라서 승무원들은 비행 중 끊임없이 돌아다니면서 손님들이 갈증을 느끼지 않도록 음료 서비스를 하도록 해야 하며, 또한 음식물은 청결하고 소화가 잘 되도록 준비된 상태에서 제공되도록 정성을 쏟아야 한다.

2) 수면의 욕구

생활리듬과 시간대가 틀린 다양한 손님들에게 있어 기내에서 편안하게 쉬고 싶어하는 수면의 욕구는 매우 중요하다. 피로한 상태로 탑승하게 된 손님에게는 식사를 하거나 영화를 보는 것보다는 그저 방해받지 않고 편안히 수면을 취하는 것이 훨씬 쾌적한 여행이 되므로 승무원들의 각별한 관심과 보살핌이 필요하다. 특히 기내의 소음, 진동, 좁은 좌석, 기압, 시차 등의 여러 가지 불편한 여건을 감안할 때 승무원들의 손님에 대한 세심한 배려가 더더욱 필요하다 하겠다.

3) 보온의 욕구

사람들은 따뜻한 상태에 있기를 바라는 보온의 욕구를 가지고 있다. 보통 기내의 최적 온도는 23도인데, 보온의 욕구를 만족시키기 위해서는 각 개인의 정도에 따르는 것이 원칙이나 온도를 어떻게 하면 전체 손님의 요구에 맞게 효율적으로 조절할 수 있겠느냐에 유의하면서 손님을 보살피지 않으면 안 될 것이다.

기내가 전체적으로 춥거나 더우면 승무원은 조정실(cockpit)에 연락하여 조절하도록 한다. 그리고 승무원은 개인의 신체적 상태에 따라 또는 손님 요구에 따라 모포를 제공한다거나 좌석 이동 등을 통하여 손님의 요구를 충족시켜 줄 수 있을 것이다.

4) 신체적 활동 욕구

사람은 본래가 활동적이어서 건강한 상태에 있는 한 끊임없이 활동한다. 그러나 손님은 기내라는 제한된 공간에서 생활해야 하므로 승무원들은 적극적으로 자주 돌아다니면서 개인적인 배려를 함으로써 손님의 활동 욕구를 간접적으로나마 충족시켜 줄 수 있도록 노력해야 한다.

5) 보살핌을 받고 싶어하는 욕구

손님들이 항공사를 선택할 때, 특히 장거리 비행의 경우에서는 승무원들의 기내 서비스수준과 내용 및 친절 등이 가장 크게 고려된다고 알려져 있다. 따라서 승무원들은 이러한 점을 명심하여 손님들을 가능한 한 친절하게 보살피도록 배려해야 할 것이다.

6) 마음의 긴장에서 해방되고 싶어하는 욕구

여행의 즐거움 중의 하나는 공무든 즐거움을 위해서든 일단 비행기에 오르면 누구나 스트레스에서 해방되어 여행의 즐거움을 만끽하려는 것이 일반적인 경향이다. 따라서 적당량의 술이나 음료로써 또는 좋은 대화를 통해 이들의 여행 분위기를 잘 이끌어 주고 즐길 수 있도록 유도해 주는 것이 승무원의 임무라 할 수 있다.

7) 안전의 욕구

모든 손님의 가장 근원적이고도 본질적인 욕구는 목적지까지 무사하고 안전하게 도착하고 싶어하는 것이다. 승무원은 손님의 이런 욕구와 기대를 항상 의식하고 비행 안전과 보안에 깊은 관심과 노력을 기울여 손님에게 신뢰와 안정감을 심어주도록 해야 한다.

8) 동등한 대우를 받고 싶어하는 욕구

손님들은 때로 승무원들이 불친절하다든가 차별대우를 한다는 선입관념을 가지고 비행에 임할 때가 있다. 특히 승무원이 외국인에게나 특정 손님에게 지나친 친절과 호의를 베푸는 것은 동등한 자격과 권리를 갖고 탄다고 생각하는 손님의 기대를 저버리고 심한 불쾌감을 주게 되므로, 기내 서비스에 있어서는 이런 점에 특히 주의를 기울여 임무를 수행토록 해야 할 것이다.

9) 인정받고 싶어하는 욕구

사람은 누구나 사랑을 받고 싶어하고, 또한 인정받기를 바라는 욕구가 강하다. 그러므로 사람은 자기가 하찮은 존재가 아닌 귀중한 사람이라는 대접을 받을 때 기쁨을 느낀다. 따라서 승무원은 손님들에게 예를 갖추어 공손하게 대하고, 이들을 칭찬을 해 줌으로써 이러한 손님들의 욕구를 충족시키도록 노력해야 할 것이다.

10) 기타 손님이 갖고 있는 욕구는 다음과 같다

기타 손님이 갖고 싶어하는 욕구에는 환영 기대심리, 독점하고 싶은 심리, 우월을 느끼고 싶은 심리, 흉내내고 싶은 심리, 손해를 보고 싶지 않은 심리, 자기 본위의 심리 등이 있다.

2. 일반적인 손님 응대 요령

1) 다양한 여행목적을 가진 손님 응대 요령

객실 승무원은 손님 개개인을 모두 동일시하며, 손님이라는 하나의 집단으로 보는 경우가 많다. 그러나 손님의 개성이 각각 상이하며, 여행목적 또한 다양하다. 그러므로 객실승무원은 항상 손님 개개인에 대해 각별한 주의와 높은 관심을 가져야 하며, 이렇게 함으로써 손님들에게 보다 좋은 서비스를 제공하게 된다.

객실승무원이 관심을 가져야 할 몇 가지 손님의 타입을 살펴보면 다음과 같다.

(1) 여성 손님

여성 손님은 일반적으로 기내 온도, 음식, 서비스에 대해 쉽게 불만을 터뜨리며, 남자 손님들에게 보다 신경을 쓰는 듯 보이는 여승무원에 대해서는 즉각적인 분노감을 나타낸다. 유아나 어린이를 동반한 여인은 남편과 같이 여행하는 부인이나 미혼녀보다 더 많은 객실승무원의 도움을 필요로 하면서도 도움을 잘 요구하지 않는 경향이 있다.

(2) 어린이

2~6세의 어린이들은 장거리 비행에도 쉬지 않고 말썽을 만든다. 이 나이의 어린이들을 다루는 데는 어린이의 부모들이 가장 효과적이므로, 경우에 따라 승무원은 어린이들이 다치지 않게 자기 좌석에 앉아 있도록 해달라고 기술적으로 부모들에게 요청할 필요가 있다.

그러나 많은 어머니들은 승무원이 그들의 어린이를 완전히 책임지고 돌보아 줄 것으로 기대하고 있는 것도 사실이다. 따라서 승무원들은 모형비행기 등의 작은 선물을 어린이들에게 제공하여 이들을 보다 용이하게 돌봐줄 수 있다.

이에 비해 7~12세의 어린이는 비교적 다루기가 쉽다. 이 또래의 어린이들은 객실 내를 뛰어 다니며 다른 손님들에게 큰 방해가 되곤 하는데, 이들을 다룰 때는 어린이를 대하는 태도를 피하고 마치 성인에게 얘기하는 듯한 말씨와 태도를 보이는 것이 효과적이다.

(3) 보호자 없이 여행하는 어린이

생후 3개월~12세까지의 보호자 없이 여행하는 어린이를 unaccompanyined minor라 한다. 이들은 일반적으로 나이에 비해 어른스러운 태도를 보이며, 스스로를 잘 돌보는 경향이 있다. 승무원은 비행기에서 내릴 때 타 손님보다 먼저 이들을 내리도록 하여 지상 직원에게 직접 인계한다.

또한 보호자 없이 여행하는 어린이들은 승무원의 말을 전부 사실인 것으로 진지하게 받아들이는 경향이 있으므로, 비행 중 농담으로 이들을 불안하게 만들거나 실현 불가능한 약속을 해서는 안 된다.

(4) 유명인사

이들은 항공여행이 잦으며, 대부분의 경우 승무원의 특별한 관심을 기대하거나 요구하지 않으며, 가능한 한 자신을 드러내지 않는 것을 더 선호한다. 따라서 승무원은 이들에게 개인적인 질문을 한다거나 사진촬영을 요구하는 등의 행동은 절대 피해야 한다.

(5) 언어불통 손님

특수 언어를 사용하여 승무원과 의사소통이 어려운 손님이 있을 경우 언어 소통이 가능한 다른 손님을 옆 좌석에 앉도록 조치해 두는 것이 좋다. 일반적으로 옆 좌석에서 통역을 해주는 손님은 자기가 할 수 있는 외국어를 사용하게 된 것을 즐거워하는 경향이 있다.

(6) 처음으로 항공여행을 하는 손님

이들은 쉽게 구별이 가능하며, 승무원은 이들이 항공여행 경험이 없음을 알고 있다는 내색을 하지 말고, 이들이 편안하게 느끼도록 대해야 한다. 예를 들어, 승무원은 손님을 교육을 시킨다는 느낌을 주지 말아야 하며, "~에 대해 가르쳐 드리겠습니다.", "이번이 첫 번째 항공여행이시죠?", "항공여행을 해보신 적이 없으시군요."라는 표현 대신 "제가 도와 드리겠습니다.", "저희 항공사를 이용하시기는 처음이신 것 같군요." 라는 표현을 사용하며, 손님의 질문에는 주변의 손님들이 이들의 첫 여행자임을 눈치 채지 않게 조용한 목소리로 확실한 답변을 하도록 해야 한다.

2) 다양한 국적의 손님 응대 요령

항공기 손님은 다양한 국적 및 인종으로 구성되어 있다. 따라서 이들은 각각 상이한 관습, 기호, 사회규범, 종교 등을 가지고 있으므로, 승무원은 이러한 모든 차이점을 숙지하고 수용할 수 있어야 한다.

일반적인 국적별 손님의 특성과 대처방법은 다음과 같다.

(1) 한국인

한국인은 국적 항공사에서 여타 외국인 손님에 비해 특별한 서비스를 받을 것을 기대하고 있는 것이 일반적인 경향이다. 따라서 승무원이 외국인 손님에게 더 많은 관심을 기울인다고 느끼면 강한 반감을 가지게 된다. 또한 이들은 자신들의 요구나 감정을 즉각적으로 표현하지 않고 망설이며, 누적시키는 경우가 많다. 따라서 승무원은 사전에 이들의 요구사항과 감정의 움직임을 파악하여 대처하여야 한다.

(2) 일본인

일본인은 정중함, 우아함, 예의 바름을 매우 중요시한다. 그러므로 승무원에게도 이와 같은 정중하며, 예의 바른 서비스를 기대하고 있다. 예를 들어, 홍차서비스 중 홍차를 옷에 쏟았을 경우 즉각 세탁 쿠폰(cleaning coupon)을 갖다 드리는 것보다는 정중하고 진실된 태도로 사과하는 것이 훨씬 더 중요하며, 그 후에도 두 번, 세 번 정중한 사과를 거듭해야 진정한 사과로 받아들이는 경향이 있다.

(3) 중국인

대체적으로 중국인은 격식을 중요시 않고, 외향적이며, 적극적이다. 또한 이들은 객실승무원에게 쉽게 접근하며, 자신의 요구를 빠짐없이 즉각 표시하여 서비스를 유도해 낸다. 객실승무원은 모든 손님에게 공정한 서비스를 제공받고 있다는 느낌을 주어야 하므로 이들에 대한 기술적인 서비스 요령이 필요하다.

(4) 서양인

이들은 개인적인 주장이 강할 뿐 아니라 응당 받아야 될 권리에 대해서는 서비스의 100% 제공을 요구한다. 서양인은 순번을 기다리고 있다가 자기의 순번이 오면 '찬스는 이때다' 하고 100% 서비스를 요구하려 든다. 또한 자기가 치른 값에 대해 당연히 받아야 할 몫을 당당히 주장한다. 예를 들면, 비행기가 정비가 필요하여 제 시간에 떠나지 못하고 지연될 때, 비행기의 결함으로 인해 목적지에 가지 못했을 때, 가방이 분실되었거나 미착되는 등 수화물에 이상이 발생할 때 서양 사람들은 자신들의 요구사항을 분명하게 표시한다. 따라서 객실승무원은 서양인들을 대할 때는 합리적인 접근방식을 취하는 것이 좋다.

3. 손님 유형별 응대법

승무원들은 기내에서 다양한 유형의 손님들을 만나게 된다. 구체적인 손님 유형별 특징과 응대요령은 다음과 같다.

손님 유형	특 징	응대요령
자기를 과시하려는 손님	•자랑이 심하고 거만하며, 자기를 과시하고 싶은 마음을 솔직히 노출한다. •하급직원 따위는 거들떠보지도 않고, 책임자에게만 접근하려 한다. •전문용어를 사용하는 등 아는 티를 낸다. •회사 고위간부와 친분을 과시한다. •적성이 풀리면 오히려 솔직한 면이 나타나 기분좋게 협력한다.	•거역하지 말고, 마음껏 뽐내게 한다. •아니꼽다 하여 절대 맞부딪치거나 무시하지 않는다. •단순한 면이 있으므로 일단 이런 사람의 호감을 얻게만 된다면 여러 면으로 이득이 되는 경우가 많다.
거만한 손님	•반발을 느끼게 하는 표정이나 태도는 심한 저항을 불러 일으켜 악순환을 되풀이하게 한다.	•말씨 및 태도를 공손히 하여 상대를 추켜 세워주고, 결코 비굴하게 보여서는 안 된다. •정중한 태도로 재빨리 응대한다.

손님 유형	특 징	응대요령
낯익은 손님		•다른 손님들이 소외감을 느낄 정도로 지나친 친절을 보이지 않도록 한다. •공사를 분명히 하고 "친한 중에도 예의가 있다"는 말과 같이 예의에 벗어나지 않도록 한다.
성급한 손님	•어떤 상황이 벌어졌을 때 제일 먼저 반응을 보이는 형태의 손님이다. •'빨리 빨리' 등 재촉이 심하며, 기다리지 못하고 '이래라 저래라' 지시까지 한다. •특히 비즈니스맨에 많으며, 쉽게 흥분하거나 과격해질 우려가 있다.	•말은 시원시원하게, 행동은 민첩하게 한다. •손님의 몸짓이나 표정, 말하는 내용에서 무엇을 기대하고 있는가를 재빨리 알아차려 먼저 응대하도록 한다.
신경질적인 손님	•아무것도 아닌 일에 매우 신경을 쓴다. •사사건건 트집을 잡아 짜증을 부린다. •말이 많고 꼬투리 잡기를 좋아한다.	•말씨나 태도에 조심하여 정중히 대하고, 상대의 불만을 제거하도록 노력한다. •작은 일에도 문제를 일으킬 염려가 있는 사람이므로 서비스시에 찻잔을 놓는다든가, 물에 무엇이 떠 있지 않는가를 잘 보고 서비스하도록 한다. •맞장구치고, 추켜세우며 설득한다. "옳습니다. 선생님은 확실히 예리하시군요." "저도 그렇게 생각하고 있습니다만…." 하고 설득한다.
의심 많은 손님	•이것저것 캐묻고 이해되기까지 질문을 계속한다.	•자신감 있는 태도로 간결 명확하게 응대한다. •애매한 설명은 물론 너무 자세한 설명이나 친절도 의심의 대상이 된다. •분명한 근거나 증거를 제시하여 스스로 확신을 갖도록 유도하고, 때로는 책임자로 하여금 응대하게 한다.
깐깐한 손님	•별로 말이 없으나 직원의 잘못은 꼭 짚고 넘어간다. •예의는 바른 편이며, 직원에게 깍듯이 대한다. •자존심이 강하므로 가장 조심해야 할 손님이다.	•정중하고 친절히 대해준다. •잘못을 지적할 때는 반론을 펴지 말고 "지적해 주셔서 고맙습니다." 하고 받아들이는 자세를 보인다.

손님 유형	특 징	응대요령
자신감이 없어하는 손님	•마음 속의 생각을 주저하며, 확실히 말하지 못한다. •여행에 익숙하지 못하거나 특별한 서비스에 익숙하지 못하다.	•안내단계에서부터 적극적이며, 자상한 태도로 대한다. •자신감을 북돋아 주는 대화를 한다. •마음이 편하도록 응대한다.
얌전 과묵한 손님	•속마음을 헤아리기 어렵다. •조금 불만스러운 일이 있어도 질 내색을 하지 않는다. 그러나 말이 없다고 해서 흡족한 것으로 착각해서는 안 된다. 말이 없는 대신 오해도 잘한다.	•정중하고 온화하게 미소를 띠고 대해 주며, 차근차근 빈틈없이 응대해야 한다.
내성적인 손님	•큰 소리나 너무 활달한 서비스는 이런 종류의 손님을 당황하게 만들고 위축시킨다.	•이쪽에서 정중하게 대화를 이끌고, 친절하고 명랑한 분위기를 만들도록 해야 한다.
말 많은 손님	•서비스의 내용이나 응대 등에 말이 많고 거친 태도를 취한다. •밑도 끝도 없이 계속 얘기한다.	•말문을 막지 말고 끝까지 경청한다. •이쪽 사정을 있는 그대로 간명하게 설명한다. •이쪽에서 가급적 묻는 역할을 하도록 하는데 "그렇습니다.", "정말", "네" 등으로 적질히 빈응을 보이고, 바쁠 때는 기분을 상하지 않도록 정중히 중단시키고 다른 일을 하도록 한다. •상대의 페이스에 말려들지 않는다. •말 많은 만큼 기분변화도 많다.
쾌활한 손님		•이런 손님에게는 너무 정중하게만 대할 것이 아니라 한 발 나아가 친숙한 사이로 접근해 봄직하다. •일을 처리함에 있어 Yes, No를 분명히 하는 것이 좋다. •상대방의 쾌활함에 말려들어 예의를 벗어나는 일이 없도록 주의한다.
추근대는 손님	•나쁜 선입견을 가지고 상식 이하의 태도로 대하거나 보기 싫게 추근거리는 예가 있다.	•이때는 적당하게 잘해주되 정도가 지나치면 절도 있고 엄격한 태도로 한계를 짓는다. 계속해서 붙잡고 놓아주지 않으면 좀 더 경험이 많은 선배승무원 또는 사무장에게 응원을 청하도록 한다. 허점을 보이면 계속 추근대기 쉬우므로 품위 있게 처신하도록 해야 한다.

손님 유형	특 징	응대요령
어린이 동반손님		•어린이에 대한 관심을 손님 자신에 대한 관심으로 여긴다. •어린아이의 특징을 재빨리 파악하여 적절한 찬사를 보내는게 효과적이다. •울거나 칭얼거린다하여 "여기서 울면 못써요"하고 윽박지를 것이 아니라, 살짝 안아준다거나 도닥거려야 재치가 있다.

참고문헌

강은주(1995). 여행영어회화 핸드북, 웰컴미디어.

고시학회(1997). 항공사 남녀 승무원.

대한항공(1997). Morning Calm, August.

대한항공 홈페이지 http://kr.koreanair.com

문홍규(1995). 항공사시험가이드, 백산출판사.

박중홍(1995). 공항은 휴식하지 않는다, 우석.

박천우(2002). 항공승무원 자질 계발, 백산출판사.

박혜정 · 방성원 · 정호정(2005). 최신 항공객실서비스실무, 백산출판사.

백선엽(1997). 책을 펼치면 미국이다 ②, 민예원.

윤대순(1997). 항공실무론, 백산출판사.

이동희 · Alan Parsons(2006). 항공실무영어, 새로미

이늑형 편저(1995). 여행자를 위한 영어회화, 이래.

이선희 · 김동헌 · 이충희 · 김인호(1996). 항공운송사업개론, 기문사.

이영희 편저(1998). 항공기 객실서비스 예절, 인하공업전문대학 출판부.

조인환 · 변동현(2001). 항공서비스영어, 백산출판사.

조화유(1994). 조화유의 미국영어 - 김선달의 미국여행기, 밝은누리.

(주)세계관광네트워크(1996). 해외여행 ABC.

차병무 · 이원용 · Kathy Garnet(1996). 항공승무원 실용영어, 명지출판사.

최혁순(1995). 필수 여행자영어, 신나라.

하헌국 · 송두석 · 안순예(1998). Modern Tourism English, 한올출판사.

황인숙(1997). 캐세이 퍼시픽의 아름다운 프로 레나, 명경.

저자소개

차석빈

저자는 1996년부터 현재까지 순천향대학교 사회과학대학 관광경영학과에 재직 중이다. 그는 고려대학교 영어영문학과를 다니는 동안 영어통역안내원 자격증을 취득하면서 관광분야와 인연을 맺게 되었다. 저자가 학부를 졸업하던 1980년대 후반, 아직 관광분야가 사람들에게 낯설게 여겨지던 무렵, 그는 관광분야에 눈을 돌려 경희대학교 관광경영학과에서 대학원 공부를 시작하였다. 그리고 좀더 넓은 관광분야를 알고자 그는 국제로터리재단 장학생으로 미국으로 건너가 Virginia Tech 환대·관광경영학과(Dept. of Hospitality & Tourism Management)에서 공부를 한 후 호텔·관광경영학 박사학위를 취득하였다.

1996년부터 그는 '여가론', '펼치면 항공영어가 보인다', '펼치면 매너가 보인다', '어디서나 즐거운 펀 펀 레크리에이션', '사례로 본 다변량분석의 이해', '관광학총론' 등의 저서를 저술하였으며, Journal of Travel Research, Journal of Hospitality & Leisure Marketing, 관광학연구, 고객만족경영연구 등 국내·외 학술지에 90여 편의 논문을 발표하였다. 또한 그는 한국관광학회 산하 호텔·외식경영분과학회 회장, 한국고객만족경영대상 심사위원 등 산학에서 활발한 활동을 하는 등 그동안 환대·관광분야에서 쌓아온 활동의 업적을 인정받아 2006년 이후 미국의 Marquis Who's Who(In the World, In America, In Asia), American Biographical Institute(ABI) 및 영국의 International Biographical Centre(IBC) 등 세계 3대 인명사전기관으로부터 인명사전에 등재 혹은 여러 상을 수상하였다.

학자로서의 삶을 천직으로 여기는 저자는 초심을 잃지 않고 꾸준히 학생들에게 변화하는 세상과 미래상을 보여주기 위해 환대·관광분야에 대한 관심과 공부를 게을리하지 않고 있다.

(개정증보)

펼치면 항공영어가 보인다 (MP3용 CD포함)

1998년 7월 15일 초 판 발 행
2007년 3월 5일 개정판 6쇄 발행
2009년 8월 15일 개정증보판 발행

저 자 차 석 빈

발행인 (寅製) 진 욱 상

발행처 백산출판사

서울시 성북구 정릉3동 653-40
등록 : 1974. 1. 9. 제 1-72호
전화 : 914-1621, 917-6240
FAX : 912-4438
http://www.baek-san.com
edit@baek-san.com

값 13,000원
ISBN 978-89-6183-210-6 (93740)